JESUS
THE WAY AND TRUTH
TO A SUCCESSFUL, HAPPY LIFE!

JESUS

THE WAY AND TRUTH

TO A SUCCESSFUL, HAPPY LIFE!

Jesus Four Steps that Lead to Peace,
Joy, True Success, and Happiness

Rick Nelson

ELM HILL

A Division of
HarperCollins Christian Publishing

www.elmhillbooks.com

Jesus
The Way and Truth to a Successful, Happy Life!
Jesus Four Steps that Lead to Peace,
Joy, True Success, and Happiness

Published in Nashville, Tennessee, by Elm Hill, an imprint of Thomas Nelson. Elm Hill and Thomas Nelson are registered trademarks of HarperCollins Christian Publishing, Inc.

Elm Hill titles may be purchased in bulk for educational, business, fund-raising, or sales promotional use. For information, please e-mail SpecialMarkets@ ThomasNelson.com.

Scripture quotations marked KJV are from the King James Version. Public domain.

Scripture quotations marked NIV are from the Holy Bible, New International Version®, NIV®. Copyright © 1973, 1978, 1984, 2011 by Biblica, Inc.® Used by permission of Zondervan. All rights reserved worldwide. www.Zondervan.com. The "NIV" and "New International Version" are trademarks registered in the United States Patent and Trademark Office by Biblica, Inc.®

Scripture quotations marked NKJV are from the New King James Version®. © 1982 by Thomas Nelson. Used by permission. All rights reserved.

Library of Congress Cataloging-in-Publication Data

Library of Congress Control Number: 2019911214

ISBN 978-1-400327256 (Paperback)
ISBN 978-1-400327263 (eBook)

Jesus
The Way and Truth
to a Successful, Happy Life!

Jesus' Four Steps that Lead to Peace,
Joy, True Success, and Happiness

CONTENTS

ACKNOWLEDGMENTS

First and foremost, I want to thank God for his abundant grace and mercy he extended to me during my years of foolish living and giving me more chances than I deserve. I also want to thank Jesus for teaching me what true success and happiness is all about. And showing me his steps in this book on how to follow his plans and purpose for my life. I need to especially thank my wife for staying married to me during the bad and ugly times having to deal with all my dysfunctional ways. I don't believe there is a woman on planet Earth that would have stuck by my side as long as you have. But that's okay; all I needed is one special woman and God gave me you. I love you with all my heart. Furthermore, I would not feel right if I did not mention the ministries of the people I believe God used to make an impact in my life in some way or another: Jack Van Impe, Charles Stanly, Rick Warren, Joel Osteen, Joyce Meyers, and Sarah Young. Thank you all and I hope the change and impact that you have made in my life will in some way extend to as many lives as possible.

INTRODUCTION

Years ago before God spoke to me about writing this book, my question was does God want us to live a successful happy life? Or is that left to us to find out on our own the best way we can? The answers to both those questions are revealed throughout this book. These are based on God's word, his promises, biblical examples, twenty-five years of bible study, and personal experiences of trying to achieve success and find happiness in all the wrong ways.

In my research, I learned the one thing that all mankind wants and can't live without aside from water and food is happiness. So I decided to study the bible from cover to cover and find out everything God had to say about being happy and successful. And I learned he not only wants us to be happy, but he also wants to fulfill the desires of our hearts—and that really captured my attention (Psalms 37:4). The catch is we have to let him show us the desires of our heart and what true happiness is, not the other way around.

The other thing I learned is God and Jesus talk more about success than they do about happiness. That's because success always precedes happiness and the definition of success is nothing more than a favorable outcome. In other words, no matter what you do or happens in your life and the outcome is not favorable, then you're not going to be happy about it.

I ask people, "If you had a choice between being happy or being successful, what would you choose?" Everybody says they'd rather be happy first and that was me too. And then I'd ask them this question, "Can you think of any scenario where you don't have a favorable outcome and you would still be happy about it?" So far no one has come up with an answer yet.My point is the more favorable outcomes you have in your life, the happier you're going to be. That's why we need Jesus: he is the true definition of success because everything he does has a favorable outcome. That's why Jesus talked more about success then he did about happiness (John 14:6, KJV). Jesus says it all in a nutshell: "I am the way, the truth, and the life."

I took Jesus up on that twenty-five years ago when I failed at trying to be successful and happy. I threw in the white towel, gave up on myself, and said, "Okay, Jesus, you show me the way to life."

And that he did: he's been showing me the way to what true success and happiness really is ever since.

Now he wants me to share that with you. That's what this book is all about: you finding Jesus and letting him show you the way to true success, peace, joy, and happiness. Jesus taught four principal steps to follow on a daily basis to living a successful, happy life. His four steps in this book will help guide and show you what he wants you to do each day. These are according to his purpose and plan which he already has prepared for you for a successful life of peace, joy, and happiness.

CHAPTER 1

How Bad Is Your Situation?

Happiness is the one thing I have found that all mankind wants, seeks, and desires. And we are willing to do just about anything to get it, even kill over it if anyone gets in our way or tries to keep us from it. I realize most of us are not going to kill someone over it, but we will do a whole lot of other bad things to get it. These include lying, stealing, abusing ourselves with drugs or alcohol trying to do what we think is going to make us happy, but all that does is make things worse. That's because the bad things we do to ourselves or other people have results called bad consequences. On the other hand, the opposite is true: the good things that we do to ourselves or other people have good consequences. In other words, God has principles and priorities we need to obey and live by if we want true happiness and success. And no matter what we do, we cannot ever change the outcomes of his principles simply because God made it that way. The bible says, *"Be not deceived, God is not mocked whatsoever a man sows that shall he also reap."* (Galatians 6:7, KJV) In other words, don't fool yourself or be fooled by the Devil and think you can break God's rules by doing something bad and have a successful outcome. That's never going to happen because God would be mocked if he allowed us to change the outcome of his rules.

I wasted a lot of years of my life trying to break that rule doing bad things and expecting good outcomes that never happened. The sooner you abide by God's principal rule of what you sow is what you reap, the better off your life is going to be. I believe there are a lot of people in bad situations they want to get out of so they can be happy. For them I hope I have covered the most basic ones in this chapter.

We all want to be happy but a lot of times we go about it the wrong ways and sometimes it's because we never learned how to go about it the right way. At least that's the way it was for me. That's why my goal is that by the time you finish this book, you will know the right way. And what changes you need to make and what you need to do to live a happy and successful life. Not the world's way, your way or my way, but according to Jesus' way. I don't believe we can be happy while we're in a bad situation; at least I never was, until God successfully got me out of it. In other words, the goal is to stay out of bad situations as long as you have the choice to do so. I believe most of the time we are the cause of why we are in a bad situation in the first place. And I said most of the time not all the time because there are bad situations that God allows to happen in our life that we have no control over and I've been in a lot of those. But most of my bad situations I caused upon myself by making wrong choices as you'll hear throughout the book. But God still turned them all around for my good. He can do the same for you. The bible says, *"We know that all things work together for good to them who love God."* (Romans 8:28, KJV)

Nothing is impossible with God

One point I want to make in this chapter is this: no matter how bad your situation is right now, God is able to change any situation you're in regardless if you caused it or not or how hopeless it looks. I know that from my own personal experience. Thirty-six years ago, I was in the most hopeless situation of my life that I will never forget as long as I live. My wife was diagnosed with a malignant tumor on the back of her brain stem when she was only twenty-two years old. The situation was when she ate food, it would go into her lung and couldn't swallow, causing her not to eat through her mouth. The doctors and specialists at our local hospital could not figure out why that was happening and what the problem was. After they had exhausted all their tests, they told me there was nothing more they could do. After they said that, I was extremely angry at them. I could not believe that they could not at least tell us what the problem was. I said, "So you're telling me you're just going to let my wife lie here and die?"

They said the only hope would be to have her immediately flown from Michigan where we live to the Mayo Clinic in Minnesota. The problem with that was you had to be flown in a small private charter plane that required $1,200 cash up front that we didn't have at the time. I didn't know what to do, so I told our pastor the situation and our church lent us the money which we later paid back. That night we flew across Lake Michigan to the Mayo Clinic. I remember it was the most terrifying experience I ever had. I always said I would never fly in a plane because I was scared of heights and flying. And here I was scared to death in a plane and flying over water on top of while my wife was barely hanging on to life. This might sound crazy but I was so scared I wished I could have traded places with my wife. At least she was drugged up and didn't know what was going on. It was a small one-engine plane. I remember asking the pilot as we were crossing Lake Michigan if the engine stopped how far could we glide. I kept asking him how close we were to land just so I would feel a little safer while I was praying to God the whole time. When we finally landed, it was the biggest relief I think I ever had. The funny thing is now I like flying. My wife always told me if God wants you dead, he doesn't have to wait till you get into a plane to do it, but that still didn't help my fear.

When we arrived at Mayo Clinic, I was told we had one of the best brain surgeons in the world. After all the testing and X-rays, the doctor took me into a room and told me the bad news. He said, "I'm sorry to have to tell you that your wife has only about six months to live. She has a malignant cancerous tumor rapidly growing on the back of her brain stem, causing her food to go into her lungs." Then he showed me the

X-rays and the tumors that you could see spreading through the back of her brain. He said the only thing that could be done was radiation treatments to slow the growth down so she could live a few more months. Even after I heard that, I believed that there was still hope that God could change the situation someway somehow. I remembered and keep saying the verse, **"For with God nothing shall be impossible."** (Luke 1:37, KJV) I didn't eat for three days. All I did was pray like I never had before and begged God to let my wife live. I had to call home and tell all my family, church family, and friends the bad news. They were all praying for a miracle to happen. She was put on a prayer chain with our church and other churches throughout our state. We were both youth leaders at the time. The third day she was scheduled for exploratory surgery to get a sample of the tumor to know how much radiation treatment she needed. After the surgery while I was in the waiting room, I could see the doctor coming down the hall. And I remember he had a big smile on his face so I looked round to see who he might be smiling at because it surely couldn't be at me. There was no one else around me and he keep getting closer with this big smile. I couldn't figure out why he would be smiling at me. That's when he said to me, "The surgery went well. In fact, your wife is going to be okay and will not need any chemotherapy." He said he took out a benign noncancerous tumor about the size of his finger and she would be ready to go home in a few days. I said, "What?" I couldn't believe what I just heard him say and asked him to please say that to me again. I was in shock. I couldn't believe what I was hearing. I said what about the X-rays when you showed me all the tumors spreading around her brain stem? How did it become a benign tumor? He said the only explanation he could give was it had to be a miracle. He said it was very rare and in his career he only saw it happen one other time.

There was no amount of words I could express how I felt that day other than I was the happiest man in the world. I had to ask him again about the chemotherapy and he repeated there was no need for it, though she would have some permanent numbness in her right hand which she still has today.

It took a while for the reality of it all to sink in and then I called everyone and told them the good news. It was the most exciting thing in the world I have ever done to tell someone you just experienced a miracle from God. The news of what happened spread throughout the Mayo Clinic hospital. The surgeon said to me, "Before you leave, there are a lot of doctors, specialists, and staff who would like to come and see your wife if that's okay with you." I said, "Sure" and he said, "There's a lot of staff and they can't all get in the room at once. So they will have to come in small groups at different times of the day if that is still okay." I said, "Sure."

I couldn't believe the number of doctors and interns coming in nonstop the whole day. They made us feel like we were celebrities or something. The funny thing is my wife was so drugged up for so long that she was the last person to realize that God performed a miracle on her. After we got back home, we got calls from people from all over that we didn't even know were praying for us. Churches asked if I would come to share our miracle story with them. I saw a lot of other lives affected by this miracle. The only problem I had with sharing this story is it's hard to tell without getting emotional when I relive it. I thought I am past that by now after all the years but I haven't. That day, Sept 28, 1982, I made a vow to God, my wife, and my family that I will never forget it as long as I live. Every year I thank God by putting roses around the house to remind us of that day. My wife has the verse from Luke 1:37, "With God nothing is impossible," tattooed on the back of her neck where the tumor was. When people see it on her neck and ask what it means, it gives her the opportunity to share her story. And ever since each year, we celebrate that day thanking God for his miracle.

The thing I learned from this experience is it is one thing to read about God's miracles in the bible and it is a whole other thing to experience it personally before your own eyes. And if there is one thing I know for sure with God it is that nothing is impossible and he still does miracles today.

This chapter is about giving hope and encouragement for all those who are in a bad or hopeless situation. And I realize it's very difficult to be happy while you're going through a bad situation. And the key thing here is going through, because I don't believe God wants us to permanently stay in any bad situation; rather, you're the cause of it or not. And I have been in both, mostly the ones I caused upon my own self. God has helped me get out of every bad or what seemed like a hopeless situation I was ever in. He can turn any bad situation around and replace it with something better than what you had before. God is in the restoration business; he can take any kind of a hopeless situation and turn it around for his glory. Always keep in mind God did not promise us a continuous happy life without any problems. But he does promise to deliver us out of all of them King David said, "**For he hath delivered me out of all my troubles**." (Psalms 54:7, KJV) "*Call upon me in the day of trouble; I will deliver you and you shall glorify me.*" (Psalms 50:15, NKJV). The apostle Paul said the same thing as David. He had all kinds of persecutions and afflictions and said the Lord delivered him out of all his troubles. Jesus says, "In this world you will have troubles. But be happy because I have successfully overcome the world and your troubles." (John 16:33) In other words, Jesus doesn't want us to live a defeated, unhappy life even in the midst of our troubles. The bible says, "*But thanks be to God, **who gives us the victory through our Lord Jesus Christ**.*" (I Corinthians 15:57, NKJV) The key to remember here is that success and happiness is only found in Jesus, not in the world or anything else. And we can still have peace and joy in the midst of our troubles knowing that Jesus has the power to overcome all of them. And no matter if you're in any kind of a bad situation or trouble right now, whether it's your health, addictions, relationship, finances, job or any other area of your life. I know it from my own personal experiences of bad situations that I had in all those areas as you will hear throughout the book. Jesus can successfully help you get through whatever situation you're going through no matter how bad it may seem. Nothing is too impossible with God. He is still in the miracle and restoration business as I know firsthand. If you put God first and trust him, he's going to turn your situation around for the better. The only thing you don't know is how, what way, and how long it is going to take him. Only

God knows that answer. It may be a few days, weeks, months or even years. What I have learned is God doesn't want you to worry or stress yourself out trying to figure it out. You overcome all that by following Jesus' four steps in the last chapters of this book. The key is to be patient, as hard as that is, and wait on the Lord for his help and perfect timing. His ways are not our ways. There are times that God will allow us to go through adversity to see how we are going to react to a situation. He tests our faith and trust in him like he did with Abraham and Isaac, and when Joseph's master's wife tried to seduce him. For without adversity in our life, how can God demonstrate his deliverance, goodness, and favor? If we all lived a trouble-free life, we wouldn't need God's help or deliverance and that's not reality. God allows adversity in our life so we will give him the glory when he helps us out of trouble like this next story.

God tests us with adversity

This story is about Joseph's life which is, in my opinion, one of the best examples in the bible when it comes to adversity and success. The full story of his life is quite long so I'm going to give the short version. If you have never read his story, that's one I would highly encourage you to read. It's one of my favorite success stories found in Genesis chapters 37–50. Joseph experienced one bad situation after another. He was wrongly accused and still found success and happiness through it all with God's help. Joseph was the youngest of eleven brothers and was highly favored by his father, which his brothers hated him for. One day God gave Joseph a dream and told him he would reign over his older brothers one day.

And when he told them his dream, they hated him for it. Why would your older siblings be happy about that? One day Jacob his father told Joseph to go check on the rest of his brothers working in the fields to see if they were okay. When the brothers saw him coming, they all conspired to kill him, to throw him in a pit and tell their father some beast had killed him. After they threw him in the pit, they saw foreigners coming in the distance. So one brother says, "It's not profitable for us just to kill him; let's

7

sell him to the foreigners." Then the foreigners brought Joseph to Egypt and sold him as a slave to the Pharaoh's captain. Meanwhile the brothers took Joseph's coat and dipped it in goat's blood and told their father some beast had killed him. Imagine you hearing this about your favorite child or someone you dearly loved. Jacob wasn't just heartbroken, he was a broken man though we know Joseph was really alive. During that time, Jacob was grieving all those years. Joseph was sold as a slave when he was seventeen years old to the captain of the Pharaoh. The bible says the Lord was with Joseph and caused him to be successful in all that he did. And his master saw that his Lord was with him and he was successful in all that he did so he made him ruler over his entire house and all that he had. And the Lord blessed the Egyptian's house for Joseph's sake and was well favored. Then there came a day when his master's wife cast her eyes upon Joseph and she asked him to have sex with her. But he refused and said, "How can I do this great wickedness and sin against God?" And she continued to tempt Joseph day by day, asking him the same thing over and over again yet he still refused her. Then there came a day when she got tired of him refusing her. So she grabbed Joseph by his garment and tried to force him upon her and he escaped, leaving a piece of his garment in her hands. So when her husband came home, she told this big lie that Joseph tried to force himself upon her while he was gone. And when she cried with a loud voice for help he ran, leaving behind his garment. When Joseph's master heard his wife's story, he was full of wrath and angry and put Joseph in prison. Then while Joseph was in the prison, the Lord showed him mercy and favor in the sight of all the prisoners and prison keeper. Then the keeper of the prison committed all the prisoners to Joseph's hands and whatsoever Joseph did, the Lord made him to prosper and have good success again. Then one day the Pharaoh had a dream that troubled him and he called all the wise men he had and they could not interpret the dream. When the chief butler heard this, he told the Pharaoh that when he was in prison with Joseph, he had interpreted a dream for him and that it came to pass. Then the Pharaoh sent for Joseph out of the prison and said to him, "I have dreamed a dream that no one can interpret. I have heard that you can understand a dream and interpret it." And when Joseph answered the Pharaoh, Joseph didn't take credit for himself. He gave God the credit, telling the Pharaoh, "It is not me but God who shall give you the answer." When Joseph interpreted the Pharaoh's dream, he was so pleased he said, "I will make you ruler over all my house, all my people, and all the land of Egypt. Only in my throne will I be greater than you." Then the Pharaoh took off his ring, put it on Joseph's hand, dressed him in the finest cloths, and put a gold chain around his neck. And he even got to ride in the second chariot behind the Pharaoh. And the rest of the story ends where he reunited with Jacob his father and the rest of his brothers.

If I could go back in time, I would have loved to be at that reunion. I can't imagine how emotional that would have been. To see your favorite loved one who you thought was dead for thirteen years must have brought out buckets of tears and joy that day. The lessons to learn in Joseph's story is God was in control and behind it all the whole time just like he can be in your life. He took a seventeen-year-old boy from the bottom of a pit left for dead and sold as a slave. In thirteen years, he was made the second most powerful ruler in the world. If that isn't success, I don't know what is. There are two key things to remember in his story: it was God who gave Joseph favor and his success, and Joseph always gave him the credit for it.

Making wrong choices cause bad situations

This next story I think is a perfect example of making wrong choices and ending up in a bad situation. It is said to be one of the most unbelievable stories in the bible. The truth is the bible is full of unbelievable stories and that's because we have a God that does unbelievable things. This story is about Jonah and the whale. It is the extreme opposite of Joseph's for making the wrong choices and ending up in the worst possible situation that one could ever imagine. Most of you already heard about this story. Unlike Joseph's, it's a short one comprising four chapters found in the book of Jonah in case you haven't read it.

The bible says one day the Lord spoke to Jonah and told him to go into Nineveh which was a great city full of wickedness. And He told Jonah to preach against their wickedness. When Jonah heard that, he didn't want to have any part of it. So he boarded a ship to Tarshis thinking he could flee from the presence of the Lord. Tarshis was in the total opposite direction of Nineveh. So the Lord sent out great and mighty wind into the sea until the ship was ready to break and sink. Then all the people on the ship were afraid and every man cried unto his God. But Jonah was sleeping down in the ship and the ship master said to him, "Why are you not calling upon your God when we're all about to die?" When Jonah didn't say anything, everyone decided to cast lots to know who was causing this evil upon them and the lot fell upon Jonah. Then they asked him what he did to cause this evil to come upon them. And Jonah said, "I fear the Lord, the God of heaven and creator of earth." And he told them why he fled from the presence of the Lord.

The truth is I believe he was scared of the people of Nineveh and he didn't believe they deserved God's forgiveness. When the men heard this, they were exceedingly afraid and said, "Why have you done this?" And they said, "What shall we do to you that the sea may be calm unto us?" Jonah said, "Cast me into the sea and the sea will be calm. It's because of me that this storm has come upon you." So they cast Jonah into the sea and the sea became calm. When the men saw this, they feared the Lord even more. The bible says the Lord had prepared a great fish to swallow up Jonah and he was in the belly of the fish for three days and three nights. Then Jonah prayed and cried unto God out of the fish's belly and described it as the belly of hell. I don't know about you, but I can't imagine being in the belly of a fish for 1 minute, much less waiting three days before praying. I think he was hoping to die but when he saw God wasn't going to let him, he started to get claustrophobia. It wasn't until Jonah came to realize that either he was going to live in the fish's belly or repent and do what God asked him to do the first time. As soon as he repented to do what God asked him, then the lord caused the fish to vomit him unto the shore and dry ground. Jonah went to Nineveh, preached the message, the people repented, and the city was spared.

I have to say Jonah is the most stubborn suicidal person I have ever read about. I often ask myself why God even dealt with his extreme stubbornness. On the other hand when I stop and think about the things I have done, I have to recant that thought and thank God for that same kind of grace, mercy, and the patience he gave Jonah.

The two key things to learn from Jonah's story is you can't run or hide from the presence of God. And you can't disobey Him by making wrong choices and expect to live a successful happy life. Jonah ended up in his bad situation, what he called the belly of hell, by not obeying God and making the wrong choice. It wasn't until he decided to make the right choice, repent, and to go in the right direction that God turn things around for him.

Maybe you're not running from God but you feel like you're trapped in a situation with nowhere to go and no possible help like Jonah. One of the first things to do is be honest and ask yourself why you are in the situation you're in. Is it because of wrong choices you have made? If yes, the quickest solution to get out of your situation regardless of what you have done or how hopeless it may seem—and it can't be any worse than Jonah's—is cry out to God and ask for His help, realizing He is your only hope to get you out of your situation. King David said, "The righteous cry and the Lord hears and delivers them out of all their troubles." And like Jonah, repent for whatever it is you did or are doing that's displeasing God. The quicker you respond to God, the quicker He will help you out of any bad situation you're in. If He did it for a selfish, stubborn old Jonah, He can do it for you. Or maybe you haven't made any wrong choices at all and the situation you're in has changed around you beyond your control. Like Joseph, maybe you're hated because of jealousy or even been wrongly accused of something you had nothing to do with. If that's your situation, one thing is for sure: God knows the truth and that's all that matters. God knows what's going on; if you just keep doing what is right on your part, He will do his part and turn things around in your favor. The bible says God is not slack concerning His promises; it's not a matter of if—it's always a matter of when. It took three days for Jonah, it took weeks for my wife's miracle, it took Joseph thirteen years—the timing is always left up to God. Our part is to be patient and wait on His hand to deliver us.

God can take our bad situation to get us to a better situation

I can personally relate to a little of both stories, especially Joseph's, where circumstances and people can change around you for the worst, in addition to being wrongly accused and ending up in a bad situation . This story is about my first job when I worked at a retail company for about fifteen years. I loved my job. I thought it was the best place in the world to work, at least the first eleven to twelve years. They actually treated you like you were a king. Then other retail companies came into the area and were paying their employees a lot less per hour so they could lower their prices. Then the company I worked for started firing their managers or putting pressure on them to make them quit so they could hire new managers at half the pay. I had a great boss for most all of those years and that ended when he quit because of the pressure; then he was replaced with a jerk. It was from that point on that I started to be in the most miserable place to work. It was like I was going to prison each day and I couldn't wait to get out. I remember coming home every day telling my wife how I hated that place and wanted to quit. But I couldn't afford to: I had a family to take care of. So I had to endure the pressure and all the stress they put on me. I'll always remember the day I walked into work and realized out of thirty managers I was the only original one left who didn't quit or was fired. That was a depressing lonely feeling and I remember looking up that day and begging God to please get me out this crazy insane place. I said, "I'll do anything just please get me out of here. I can't take it anymore." Then one day I had a party at my house. It was not a work party but there were some people from the company I worked for that I invited. It was BYOB: I did not provide any alcohol and there was one employee—who was under twenty-one—drinking from what he brought or someone gave him. His mother found out, called the company, and made a complaint that I supplied the alcohol to her son which was false. The next day I was called into the office and terminated for misconduct off the job. Their own company policy stated you can only be fired for misconduct if you're on company property or company time of which I was neither. I filed a wrongful discharge suit against the company but was denied because of my incompetent lawyer who failed to file on time. So then I started my own cleaning business called Pride Janitorial Services. I named my business Pride because that was what I was full of at the time. I had so much bitterness and anger towards my employer and lawyer that I can't even express it. I'll tell you this much: I did express it to my boss who fired me and then I was not allowed on the company's property until he left that store and I was no longer a threat. I just about destroyed myself over it by abusing alcohol and drugs—if it wasn't for God's grace and mercy keeping me alive. On top of all that bitterness and anger, I was full of pride. I didn't know it then as I do now pride is the number one thing on God's hate list. So the combination of bitterness, anger, and pride was a recipe for disaster. This in turn caused me to make all kinds of foolish mistakes trying to prove I was successful. Instead I ended up in bankruptcy, losing everything except my family and my house. In addition to that, I got two DUIs within a year and one drug offence, ended up in jail, and forced to go to rehab for thirty days. As I look back on this now thirty years later, I can say that was one of the best things that happened to me. You might be saying, "That doesn't sound like a good situation; sounds more like a bad situation."

Back then it was a bad situation for a while but it gradually turned into a better one. I call it the turning point in my life when God started his restoration process. Like Jonah I was forced by God to stop and take a good hard look at my life and the direction I was going. Jail and rehab stopped me in my tracks because I was headed down the wrong road of self-destruction without realizing it. I was my own man full of pride and calling my own shots. I thought I knew what was right for my life and was going to do things my way. I was going to be in control of my destiny. I wasn't going to let anybody have the power to fire me again. This was during a period of my life which spanned about twelve years, mostly in my thirties. I was actually destroying myself trying to find happiness and success doing it my way without God. I thought I was having fun but not without paying the price of bad consequences. My life was full of turmoil. And that's the Devil's plan: to make you think you're having fun while he's behind the scene causing chaos and destruction in your life. The sad part is you're giving him permission to do it by making the wrong choices. That's why Peter says, "Be sober and alert because your adversary the Devil is walking around seeking who he can destroy," and I was one of them. During my time in rehab, the hardest part for me was to start being honest with myself and admit I was responsible for my actions. Instead I was blaming everyone else for the situation I was in. So that's when I started to take a real honest look at myself and evaluate my priorities and what kind of person I want to be. That's when I decided to get my priorities in the right order by putting God first in my life instead of me. For me this was the lowest point in my life. I felt like I was at the bottom of a pit. In bankruptcy for seven years with no driver's license for two of those years, court fines, I was in a financial mess. I remember saying to my wife, "How in the world are we going to live without credit cards or loans?" Actually that was part of the problem that got us into bankruptcy in the first place; the other part was me. There is a positive thing about being at the bottom of the pit: you can't go any farther down; all you can do is look up and call on God for help. King David said, "*He also brought me up out of a horrible pit, out of the miry clay, and set my feet upon a rock, and established my steps.*" (Psalms 40:2, NKJV)

And that's what I did. I didn't have anything to lose. That's the day I prayed to God and admitted I screwed up and asked him to help me get out of my mess. I gave up trying to do things my way and for the first time in my life I surrendered my will to God. In other words, I threw in the white towel. That's when I started to put God first in my life, listening to him and his direction. That's when I begin reading God's word and promises and claiming them for myself and going back to church. One of the first things God told me to do was change the name of my business Pride and then sell what was left of it and that's what I did. Then he had me start a new business called Image Stain Removal. He had me name it Image to remind me I needed to get the pride out my life and start a new image. Then I took God up on his promise when he said, "I am the Lord your God, who teaches you to profit, who leads you by the way you should go." (Isaiah 48:17, NKJV) I said, "Okay, show me how and I will follow," and have been doing it for over twenty-five years now. For me and for now, it's been the best job in the world because God is my direct boss and the best part is I don't have to worry about him being replaced. The only one who can replace God in your life is yourself with something else will talk more about that later in the book. The bottom line in all these stories is God can take any kind of bad situation you're in. And turn it around and give you a better situation than you had before. He took Joseph from the bottom of a pit and made him the second most powerful ruler in the world. God took my wife's malignant brain tumor and turned it into a benign one by a miracle. He took Jonah from trying to commit suicide and gave him a second chance. He took me from a job I was miserable in and hated and gave me the best job I've ever had. If it wasn't for God allowing me to have a boss who was a jerk and got me fired, I would have been a lot longer in that miserable situation because I'm not a quitter. God had better plans for me, although it didn't seem like it at the time. Now many years later I can look back and see how God was behind it the whole time. I believe everyone has bad situations happen in their life be it from a relationship, job, finances, or health. That's why I thought it was important to start the book out with how bad your situation is. That's because I was in a lot of them and way too many to even mention. The point is when we're in a bad situation it's hard to be happy, so a lot of people turn to drugs and alcohol to suppress it as I did, and that only makes things worse. And the sad reality of it all is that a lot of people get stuck right there and never make it out alive. And if it wasn't for God's grace and mercy, I and my wife would have been one of them. The truth is we both should have been dead five to six times; one of those times you already know about. The older I get, the more I realize the only thing that makes any sense about why we're still here is that God has a purpose and plan for us, and part of that plan is to tell our story to help others find true happiness and success Jesus's way. But before that can happen and if you're someone who's in a bad situation right now, the first thing you need is hope and encouragement, and that only comes from God and His help. On the other hand, the Devil wants us to feel hopeless and stay in that condition. The truth is the only ones who are in a hopeless situation without the possibility of help is the Devil, his demons, and those who reject Jesus. In other words, as long as he can get us to believe we're in a hopeless situation, we are allowing him to control our life by getting us to make wrong choices and do bad things. I don't know you or how messed up your life is or how hopeless it may look, but I do know God can take your mess and turn it around into a message for His glory to help others like He has done with me. The first step is affirming that you are ready and willing to allow God to give you a makeover and change your life for the best. I hope your answer is yes because that's what this book is all about.

This book isn't just about encouragement, God's promises, and a few success stories. It's about getting right with God and how to stay right with God by following his priority steps on a day-to-day basis. It will help you keep the Devil off your back and stop listening to him. It will show you how to listen to God and follow His plan and purpose He has for your life. It will show you how to experience His true success, peace, joy, and happiness in your life. In other words, my goal by the end of this book is not to leave you with these questions I always had: What do you do next after you surrender your life to God? How do you know what God's purpose and plan is for your life and how to follow it?

Can you relate to any of these bad situations?

Do you feel like you're at the bottom of a pit with no help? If yes, the good news is God is your help. He is all you need and He doesn't want you to stay there either. He wants to lift you up and turn your situation around so you will have a success story to tell others and glorify God with.

If you're in that situation, do what David did—who had more problems and trouble than anyone of us will ever have. The bible says he cried unto the lord and He heard his cry. And He lifted him up out of a horrible pit and miry clay and set his feet on solid ground and established his steps.

Have you been wrongly accused of something you didn't do? If yes, stay in faith. God knows the truth and that's what matters most. He's the ultimate judge. Just keep doing the right thing and putting God first like Joseph did. The scripture says God was with him and delivered him out of all his afflictions even when he was wrongly accused. (Acts 7:9, 10) Eventually God will turns things around and make things right to your favor like he did for Joseph.

Are you hated because of jealousy or envy from family or others? If yes, Jesus said, "Don't feel alone; the world hated me before it hated you and they hated me without a cause." Jesus says we're to love our enemies and those who hate us. Look at Joseph's situation: he had eleven brothers who hated him and he never hated them back once or sought any revenge. Instead the scripture says he loved his brothers and God blessed him for it; in the end, they had a big loving reunion. The lesson here is we can't control how others think or treat us. But we can control how we think and treat others and that's the key. Don't let others rob you of your joy and happiness.

Do you feel like you're enslaved or trapped by circumstances beyond your control? If yes, I know how that feels—that's how I felt in my job. The thing to remember is God is in total control, not your circumstances or the people around you. Look what God did for Joseph who was a slave and prisoner. God took me from a miserable job situation to the best job in the world. He can do the same for you. It's just a matter of time. Be patient and wait on God. He's always on time and never late.

Are you in the situation you're in because you've been making wrong choices like Jonah?
If yes, I hate to admit it but I have a lot of experience in this area: the

quickest solution is stop making the wrong choices by getting on the right road which we'll talk about next. And do what Jonah did: repent and cry out onto God. Tell him you're tired of making wrong choices and the bad situations you caused. And that you're going to start listening to God to make right choices. The minute Jonah repented is when God delivered him out of his torment and the belly of hell as he described it.

Warning! If you are going through any kind of a bad situation right now, don't make the mistakes like I did and abuse alcohol, drugs, or any other kind of vice to cope with it. I can assure you all that's going to do is make things worse, robbing you of peace and joy. Instead, take God up on his promises in this book and start enjoying the successful, happy life he has planned for you.

God's promises to remember

• Behold, I am the Lord, the God of all flesh **is**
there anything too hard for me? (Jeremiah 32:27, NKJV)

• For with God nothing shall be impossible.
(Luke 1:37, KJV)

• Call unto me, and I will answer you and show
you great and mighty things which you do
not know. (Jeremiah 33:3, NKJV)

CHAPTER 2

TWO ROADS TO TRAVEL: WHICH ONE ARE YOU ON?

Each day when we wake up God gives us a new day and the freedom to make new choices in our lives if we want to. I believe one of the most important ones to make is choosing what road you're going to travel down. In other words, we're all walking and traveling somewhere in this life but Jesus simplifies it by narrowing it down to only two roads. And in this chapter, we'll be discussing those two roads Jesus warns us about. In Matthew 7:13, 14, He says, *"Enter through the narrow gate, for wide is the gate and **broad is the road that leads to destruction,** and many enter through it. But small is the gate and **narrow the road that leads to life** and **only a few find it.**"* In other words, Jesus is telling us there are only two roads to travel: a wide road that leads to destruction and a narrow road that leads to a successful life. Jesus isn't talking about a literal road; he's talking about a spiritual road, using it as an example for us to look at. In my opinion, this part of scripture can be taken two ways. Some people can interpret the wide road leads to hell and the narrow road leads to heaven. But I don't believe that's what Jesus was trying to tell us here. However, the bible says "Because one-man sinned Adam than sin entered into the world so then death and hell passed upon all men." In other words, that's saying we are all born on that spiritual road that leads to destruction and hell if we don't accept Jesus as our Lord and savior. The bible says, "*For the wages of sin is death; but the gift of God is eternal life in Jesus Christ our Lord.*" (Romans 6:23, NKJV) In other words, I believe salvation is a one-time free gift from God when you accept his son Jesus as your personal savior for eternity, period. I haven't read anywhere in the bible that salvation is a road you travel down or that leads to heaven. Here's what I believe Jesus is saying about the wide road that leads to destruction.

The wide road is the world's road or Devil's road and whosoever lives their life on that road will ruin and destroy their life. And there's going to be many people who will choose to go that way. I believe one of the reasons for that is what the bible says in Proverbs 14:12, NKJV, "*There is a way that seems right to a man, but its end is the way of death.*" In other words, we naturally think our way is the best way to go but the bible says those ways end in death; in other words, separation from God. Jesus says there's only one way and one road that leads us to a successful happy life, and that's through him. The sad part is there's only going to be a few that find it. That's because the majority are going to try to find it on the world's wide road. Jesus' road is narrow because he knows there's not going to be a lot of Christians who will choose to live their life on it. My question is why is the wide road to a destructive life more popular than the narrow road that leads to a successful life? There's even a popular song promoting it. You may have already heard it, "Highway to Hell." That might even be the Devil's theme song after I read the lyrics. I don't know how anybody would want to sing along with that song. Even during my wild party days, that's one song I just couldn't sing along with or dance to. Unless you really believe the lyrics that hell is going to be one big party and all, your friends are going to be there too. If anyone believes that, I would suggest you read what the bible has to say about hell. The weeping and the gnashing of teeth being tormented day and night forever and ever doesn't sound like a fun party to me. The first thing Jesus wants us to know is the wide road is owned by the Devil. And how do we know that? Simply because Jesus won't lead us down a road to destruction; only the Devil does that. He's the prince of this world; this earth is his kingdom for now, that's why the bible says God is going to destroy it one day. The Devil has a lot of things in this world to deceive us with. For example, there are the lust of the flesh, the lust of the eyes, and the pride of life, wealth, fame, money, and power. That's the world's menu for happiness and success, and it's very attractive. That's what the majority of the people want, and I wanted the very same thing. That's why the Devil's road is wider and more popular than Jesus' narrow road. And the Devil knows he only has so much time to get as many people down that road as he possibly can. That's why the song says the person is on the highway to hell because a highway is wider and faster than all other roads. The sad part is there are a lot of Christians today living their lives traveling on that road. If you're a Christian, the bible says you won't lose your salvation but you sure can ruin your life and rob yourself of true happiness on it. I know that for fact because I lived my life traveling on that road for many years as a Christian. The other question I had is why is Jesus' road so hard to find? Here are some of the reasons why I believe that is the case.

First, the narrow road that leads to a successful happy life requires listening and following Jesus. That there is going to eliminate a lot of people right from the get-go. Why? Because they want to find happiness and success their own way like I did. And that's a big problem because Jesus says, "I am the only way to that true life." The other reason his road is narrow and less popular is it's all about investing your life into his kingdom instead of our own. And that is going to eliminate a lot of people because of our selfish nature. We want everything here and now; we don't like to wait for anything. The last reason is we can't see the things God has in store for us in his kingdom like we can the things of this world. That's why we have to live by faith because it is the substance of the things we hope for that we can't see or touch yet. The bible says, "*The eye has not seen nor ear heard, nor have entered into the heart of man, the things which God has prepared for those who love him.*" (I Corinthians 2:9, NKJV) I always wondered why God doesn't at least let us take a little peek at what he has prepared for us. In my opinion, the reason is if he allowed us to take even a little peek of the things he has prepared for us, we would be so consumed by what we've seen that we would not be able to even function and commit suicide to get there sooner. After seeing what God has prepared for us, this world would seem to us like a junkyard. On the other hand, if he did give us a sneak preview, then we wouldn't need faith anymore because we have already seen it. Then it would be a lot easier to invest into our real future eternal life and God's kingdom. I don't believe anyone who chooses to sacrifice the things of this world for the things of God is one day going to see heaven for the first time and say, "Oh man, this stinks! I should have enjoyed the world more!" That might sound funny, but there's a lot of Christians who don't want to live by that kind of faith which narrows the road even more. Now, are you starting to see why Jesus' road is unpopular and narrow compared to the Devil's wide road? We need to realize the Devil is the best salesman in the world because he knows all of our weaknesses and just what to fill it with. The lust of the flesh, the lust of the eyes, and his favorite, the pride of life—the one that cost him his job. Watch out for the pride of life because he knows that's the number one thing God hates. In Proverbs 6:16, 17 it says there are six things that God hates.

The first one is pride. I learned the hard way about pride, which means you don't need God or his approval. And here I once named my business after that because I was full of it. And when we don't heed to God's approval, then the Devil can sell us on everything in his world he has to offer. On the other hand, Jesus tells us all we need is him and his kingdom. In other words, we are the buyers and God allows us to make a choice of whose kingdom you're going to buy into: yours or his. Remember the Devil is always going to be running red light specials 24/7. That's why his road is wide because of the number of people running to it every day. On the other hand, Jesus doesn't have to do that. Why? Because he is the ultimate special: he has all that we need to live a successful, happy life. The sad thing is the majority of the people are getting sucked into the red-light specials that leads to an unhappy destructive life. The point I believe Jesus was warning us about the world's road that leads to destruction is this:

the Devil's road is easy to see because it has all the glitz and glamor of the things of this world that the majority of the people, including Christians, want. On the other hand, Jesus' narrow road is going to be hard to see. Why? Because Jesus doesn't promote or advertise the things of this world. That's why he doesn't need a wide road. The bible says, *Do not love the world or the things in the world. if anyone loves the world the love of the father is not in him. For all that is in the world the lust of the flesh, the lust of the eyes, and the pride of life is not of the father but is of the world. And the world is passing away, and the lust of it, **but he who does the will of God abides forever.***" (I John 2:15–17, NKJV) In other words, God is warning us ahead of time the Devil and this world he created is going to be out of business one day. And anything you bought or invested your time into here is going to be destroyed with it. On the other hand, Jesus is never going out of business—His kingdom is going to last for eternity. Then why is Jesus' road narrow, unpopular, and hard to find?

I believe the answer is Jesus' road to a successful happy life has signs with limits, warnings, and rules.

Plus Jesus says we need to wait, be patient, listen, and follow him and he will direct our path.

In other words, if we want to find true peace, joy, and success, we have to follow Jesus on his road. And why is that so unpopular? The answer for that is easy. Think about when you were a child: did you like waiting on your parents for something and having to listen and follow them? I don't know about you but I hated it and I believe most of us do. That's why the Devil's wide road is so popular. The Devil's road has big signs all over this world you can't miss. On top of that, he's got his biggest and best sign right in front of Jesus' narrow road, with flashing lights all around it. And it says, "This way to the road of happiness and success," with big flashing arrows pointing to his road. That's one reason Jesus' road is so hard to find. The Devil doesn't want us to see it and points us in his direction. Then when we get to his road, his sign says, "Welcome all! To happiness and success! Don't need a passport or any identification. Everyone is welcome, and this road only has one rule: that is, there are no rules here. Do whatever you want as much as you want and when you want and have fun." Now be honest and ask yourself which road sounds more appealing to you? Or try this for fun if you have kids at home, especially teenagers. The next time you go away and they're staying home alone, tell them you are running an experiment giving them only one rule: there are no rules this time and you can do whatever you want. And then look at the expression on their faces light up. What normal kid is not going to think that's the best thing they've ever heard? Of course, when you tell them you're just kidding they'll be pretty bummed out. But then it will give you the opportunity to explain to them why the Devil's road is so appealing in life and why we need Jesus' rules and limits. Notice on the Devil's road there's no limits, no warnings, and no rules; that's why it ends in destruction. That's the only part he doesn't advertise or wants us to know about. On the other hand, Jesus tells us the truth about both roads and how they end. That's why he has limits and rules to warn us of danger and consequences of the Devil's road. If we didn't have limits rules and warnings in our daily life, we'd be living in a chaotic mess like the Wild West days.

For example, imagine what it would be like if the roads we travel down each day didn't have speed limit, yield, caution, and stop signs. I think we all know the answer: there would be a lot more destructive accidents and deaths and that's not success. The signs and rules are there for our protection and safety. In other words, whenever you get to your destination safely, that's a favorable outcome called success. If that's the case, then why are we so reluctant to live and travel on Jesus' narrow road to the successful happy life?

Are you trying to find success and happiness on the wrong road?

Have you been trying to find success and happiness your way and nothing seems to be working out the way you want? That's a good sign you may be on the wrong road and should be pretty easy to figure out when there are only two roads. I believe there are a lot of Christians who think they're living on the right road without realizing they're really on the wrong road. In other words, you can know all about God, read your bible, go to church, be a Sunday school teacher, pastor or priest, and still be living on the wrong road. We see and hear about those kinds of stories in the news all the time. Why is that? I believe the answer is because we're being deceived by the best salesman in the world—the Devil. He is so good he can get us to believe we can have success and happiness on both Jesus' road and his road at the same time. Anyone who really believes that must also believe Jesus and the Devil will be sitting next to each other in heaven. Doesn't that sound ridiculous? That's because it is ridiculous yet we still try to do it anyway. Why is that? The only logical answer is we get duped into believing the Devil telling us somehow we can get away with it. There's a TV show I used to watch called "I Almost Got Away with It." Some of them successfully got away with the crime they did for years but ultimately, they all got caught. And the whole time they were constantly on the run, always looking behind their back. In other words, the best outcome we can ever have living on the Devil's road is almost getting away with it. That's not success or a happy way to live. On the other hand, when we live on Jesus' road he always makes sure we have favorable outcomes because he's behind it. Here's a physical literal way to look at it: can you drive your car down two roads at once? Of course not; it's ridiculous and physically impossible because you have to choose one or the other. Jesus tells us it is spiritu-ally impossible to travel on both roads and live a successful happy life. In Revelation 3:15, 16, he says, "I know your works that you are neither cold nor hot and I wish you would be one or the other. So then because you choose to be lukewarm and neither cold nor hot, I will spit you out of my mouth." In other words, Jesus is saying we can't have the best of both roads: choose one or the other. I believe there are Christians who purposely try to live their lives that way and those who took a wrong turn somewhere in their lives like I did. For example, have you ever been driving and took a wrong turn especially in busy traffic and Google didn't give you the right direction? You're out of town, don't know where you are, and you're in a hurry to get to your destination. That happens to me now and then when

I travel out of town. I hate that when it happens. I get extremely frustrated when Google screws up. Because now I'm on the wrong road heading in the wrong direction and getting farther away from my destination. So now I have to try to find someone who knows the area and ask them what's the quickest way for me to get back to the right road I need to be on. That same situation can easily happen in our life as Christians. Somewhere we make a wrong turn. And unlike the example I just gave, a lot of times we don't stop and ask for help with directions or how to get back on the right road. And we just keep traveling down that road till we can't go any farther until it ends in destruction. That was my situation years ago. I took a wrong turn literally and spiritually in my life. When I first started out in our marriage, I chose not to drink alcohol or do drugs for about the first eight years. Went to church every Sunday, and I and my wife were youth leaders as I said earlier. I was on the right road and life was good during that time and I didn't get in trouble or end up in jail. Long story short, the Devil started talking to me without me even realizing it. He started saying stuff like, "All you do is work hard. You're not really happy because you're not having any fun. Look at what everybody else is doing." It wasn't long before we stopped going to church altogether. God went from being first in my life to me being first. That was where I took the wrong turn. Then we started hanging around with old friends again to have fun, started back drinking which eventually led to drugs and wild parties. And before I knew it, I was living on the wrong road, the highway to destruction. If I told you all the destructive stories about me and my wife living on the wrong road, that would take up most of this book. And you would probably ask two questions: how in the world did you stay married and how are you still alive? There's only one answer to that: by the grace of God.

Then I started to drink hard liquor to excess mostly on weekends, which almost always ended up in some kind of destructive outcome. I actually thought it would somehow make me happier than I was and that's where I was deceived. I was trying to find happiness and achieve success while abusing alcohol and drugs. All I found was trouble and problems, which ruined many years of my life. I ended up in jail six different times because of alcohol, drugs, and fights. I was living on the Devil's road to an extreme. I never wanted to end up in jail; I was just bound and determined to find happiness and success my way without realizing I was living on the wrong road trying to find it. I'm just glad to be alive and grateful that Jesus stopped me in my tracks and knocked me off my horse many years ago. And one of those times I was literally going down the wrong road in the wrong direction. I had just left the bar. I was by myself, had way too much to drink. I should have not been driving. When I pulled out of the parking lot, I turned the wrong way, the opposite direction where I live. I was so intoxicated I didn't know where I was and pulled over on the side of the road heading in the wrong direction. I shut off the car and passed out until I was woken by a police officer knocking on my window asking me where I was going. The next thing I remember I was in jail for my second drunk driving in one year. That's when the judge said, "You got a problem" and sent me into rehab where my fork-in-the-road experience took place. That's when I started to look at my priorities. I knew I was on the wrong road because things in my life were just progressively getting worse. The sad part was it wasn't just me: I was taking my family with me and that's as selfish as it gets. I made a decision back then I needed to start putting God back in my life before I totally ruined it for me and my family. I simply just started asking God to show me what I needed to do to get back on the right road. And that didn't happen overnight for me: it took many years. The most important thing is not necessarily where you are on the right road. It's the fact that you are on the right road that matters most Why? Because that's Jesus' road; that's where you're going to find the good life he has planned for you. I can assure you that you won't find that out on the other road. If you're someone who's tired of living on the wrong road and you want to get on the right road, I hope this book and my experiences will help you do that and most importantly Jesus will. You will hear me talk and warn you a lot about the Devil along the way because of the amount of time I spent listening to him living on his road. Don't think he's just going to let you walk off onto Jesus' road without a fight and him tempting to get you back. The good news is the bible says we can beat the Devil because greater is Jesus that is in you than the Devil that is in the world. And there is only one way to beat the Devil: that's to use God's word on him the same way Jesus did. That's why it is vitally important to know it and how to use it. I will talk more about that later in the book but for now in Ephesians 4:27, it says, "Don't give place to the Devil." In other words, don't give the Devil a foothold in your life to attack you. Whatever your weakness is, that's where you get deceived or attacked the most. If you're trying to quit some bad habit, make sure you slam that sin door all the way. Because if you don't and try to close it slowly, the Devil is going to stick his foot in the door of your habit and keep it open. And once the doors open, he's going to squeeze right back into your life again, causing the same problems. In other words, don't set yourself up if you're serious about quitting whatever that is. That means get rid of everything that tempts you, otherwise you're just giving him a foothold. That's why it took me over twenty-five years to quit a bad habit: I always keep the door open a crack just in case. In other words, whether you have a little or big bad habit, it doesn't matter: they're still bad habits and not approved by God. What I mean about keeping the door open a crack is: are you keeping a little of something off to the side just in case you want to come back to it at some point? Like a vice or relationship, I can tell you that's not going to work and it's no way to break a bad habit whether big or small. Sometimes the small ones are usually the hardest to break, because we justify it as being small. And if that's what you're doing, it's not in secret. God sees it as does the Devil. The Holy Spirit and the Devil will remind you of it until you completely get rid of it. The Devil knows when you're serious or not, especially when you slam the door on his foot. What I learned about the Devil and his schemes is he will always remind you how good the times were especially when you're trying to quit. He'll say something like this: "Do you really want to quit right now? Think about how it made you feel. Don't you think you should wait a little while you still got plenty of time?" I know that all too well because he sold me on that line for many years. He's very cleaver. He always reminds you about the good feeling part, but he never reminds you about the consequence part that goes along with it. That's why he is the father of lies: it always ends in chaos, destruction, or a bad consequence. That's why he is a master at selling and the world's best salesman. Ask yourself who do you think is a better salesman, the Devil or Jesus? Do you see what I'm saying? Jesus doesn't tempt, deceive, or sell anything to anyone, that's why his road is narrow. He tells the truth, warns us of the consequences, what the end results are going to be, and a lot of people don't want to hear that. Look at how the Devil tried to tempt Jesus in Matthew 4:8–11 when he took him up to a high mountain and showed him all the kingdoms of this world and all its glory. He told Jesus, "I have the power to give you all of these things if you will just bow down and worship me" and Jesus told him to hit the road. Jesus slammed the door on him by quoting God's word. He said, "It is written that thou shalt worship the Lord thy God, and him only shall we serve." And that's the same thing that we need to do if we want to get the Devil off our back. The Devil tried to sell everything he had the power to give just to get Jesus to worship him. It didn't work because he knows the truth and the end results. Jesus knew his kingdom was not of this world. His purpose was to save us from it and show us his. The bottom line: don't be deceived by the Devil, believing his lies that you can find true happiness and success living your life on his road.

Have you had a fork-in-the-road experience?

The apostle Paul had a fork-in-the-road experience when he was traveling down the wrong road. And he actually thought he was on the right road doing God a favor and service persecuting the Lord's disciples and Jesus' followers by putting them in prison. Until he ran into Jesus one day on the road to Damascus and Jesus had to knock him off his horse to get his attention. Jesus said to him, "Saul why are you persecuting me?" Saul said, "Who are you, Lord?" And the Lord said, "I am Jesus who you are trying to persecute and it is hard for you to kick against the pricks." When Saul heard that he trembled and said, "Lord what will you have me to do?" Jesus told him to get up and start walking into the city and there he will be told what the Lord wanted him to do. When Saul got up, he realized he couldn't see: the Lord blinded him for three days so all he could do was listen to Jesus' instructions. After three days, Jesus gave him his sight back he was saved, baptized, and given a mission. Paul went from being used by the Devil on the road of destruction persecuting and destroying believers' lives to living and traveling on Jesus' road. His new mission was successfully saving people's lives for Jesus' kingdom instead of destroying them. Paul did a 180-degree turnaround, wrote more than half of the New Testament, and lived a successful happy life on Jesus' road until his end. There are a few things to notice in Paul's fork-in-the-road conversion experience.

First, he knew all about God. He just didn't know Jesus. He thought he was on the right road doing the right thing. The Devil doesn't care how much we know about God as long as we don't listen to and follow Jesus. Notice what Jesus said after he blinded him and knocked him off his horse: "It is hard for you to kick against the pricks." To me that sounds pretty painful like kicking a cactus with your bare foot. Who in their right mind would want to do such a foolish thing? In other words, Jesus is saying when we go down the wrong road, we're going against him and all you're doing is hurting yourself. The Devil is trying to destroy you and your happiness at the same time you're going against Jesus. I know one thing: I never want to be on that road ever again. Sometimes Jesus has to stop us in our tracks and knock us off our horse to get our attention like he did with Paul. He does that when he sees we're going down the wrong road and he knows we won't turn around on our own. He only does that because he loves us and has a greater plan and purpose for our life. He can't show us that while we're living on the wrong road.

Jonah was another one who had a fork-in-the-road experience as we discussed earlier. His experience was a little different from Paul's. Jonah knew he was on the wrong road and purposely headed in the wrong direction. I believe there's a lot of Christians whom Jesus has called doing the same thing as Jonah, running from God in the wrong direction. That could be you and God has called you to do something and you're trying to ignore him by living on the wrong road. The truth is we can't run from God for very long but the Devil gets us to believe somehow we can. If we don't heed his calling and turn around, he usually has to do something drastic in our life—in order to get our attention to stop continuing in the direction we're heading like he had to do with Jonah, Paul, and myself. That can all be avoided when we listen and follow Jesus on his road. Before I close this chapter, I want to share with you the lessons I've learned in my life about the two roads. Because I have lived my life with equal amount of time on both, I had to learn the long hard way that the longer you stay on the wrong road, things don't get better: they just get worse. That's why Jesus says it's a road that leads to destruction and that's exactly what happens whether we want to believe it or not. On the other hand, I have learned that living on the right road leads to a successful happy life that just keeps getting better. And just because majority of the people are going one way doesn't mean it's the right way. For example, look what happened to the majority of the people in the world in Noah's day. According to the bible, they were all living life on the wrong road except for Noah and his family who were on that narrow road. And look what finally happened: all the people except for Noah's family were destroyed in the flood. As for Sodom and Gomorrah, the bible says all those people living there were doing the same thing except for Lot and his family. What happened? God destroyed the city and all the people, even Lot's wife because she didn't want to give up that road and longed to head back. She was instantly destroyed and turned into a pillar of salt.

Here's what I believe Jesus is trying to point out to us about the two roads: that the majority of people are going to choose the things of this world, which is the wide road that leads to a destructive life. And there is only going to be few people who will find Jesus' narrow road that leads to a successful happy life. If you want to be one of those few people, the first step is be honest and ask yourself: what road do you want to live on? This is where it all started for me, being honest with myself and facing the reality of the truth which I call the fork-in-the-road experience. I found that when you know the truth, it's easier to make the right decision. God allows the Devil to twist, turn, and dilute it but the one thing he can't do is change it. In other words, Jesus is the truth and he said there's only one way to live a successful life and that's on his road.

Here is one of my favorite verses that promises a successful happy life and peace especially if you have a family: Psalms 128 says, "**Blessed is everyone who fears the Lord, who walks in his ways.** *When you eat the labor of your hands. You shall be happy, and it shall be well with you. Your wife shall be like a fruitful vine like in the very heart of your house. Your children like olive plants all around your table. Behold thus shall the man be blessed who fears the Lord."* I don't know how more blessed you can get than that. But there's a catch to that. It says blessed is everyone who walks in his ways; that means you have to be on the right road walking with Jesus. When you start making that a daily habit, that's one habit you don't want to break or give up. I can assure you God keeps all his promises when we obey his rules and principles. I don't' know what road you're living and traveling on, but I know you, God, and the Devil know. Maybe you're someone like I was: started out on the right road and for whatever reasons God's no longer a top priority in your life like he once was. And for whatever reason you took a wrong turn and ever since things haven't been going right in your life. Or maybe you're someone who's never been on the right road in the first place and you're tired of living that way and you're ready for a new change and want to start seeing God's blessings in your life. That was me twenty-five years ago: tired and ready for a new change, and if you're ready, that's all that counts. And it all starts with your choice to put God first in your life, not second or third. Then start claiming Psalms 128—that's what I did. God will bless you in all those areas as he promised as long as you walk in his ways. Then have that fork-in-the-road experience like Paul who started listening to Jesus for new direction and instructions for his life. If you're someone who's ready to make that fork-in-the-road experience, I can tell you this: you won't forget it. That's why you will hear me mention it throughout the book, because that's where it all started for me in rehab. There's no better feeling than to know that you're on the right road heading in the right direction.

And here's the best thing God has shown me in this high-tech age we live in: Jesus is always going to be the best GPS resource you can ever have. He never makes mistakes giving you the wrong directions. The bottom line is we can't live and travel on the wrong road and expect God to bless our life with peace and happiness. We can fool other people some of the time, but we can never fool ourselves, God, or the Devil. That's why he will expose our sin at every turn with a cactus at every one of them. All the years I've been living on Jesus' road listening and following him, I haven't seen a cactus or jail cell. If you're not already on that road, my hope and prayer is that you make today the turning point in your life. If you already know the Lord as your savior, simply pray something like this: "Jesus, I know I've been living on the wrong road trying to find happiness my way and nothing works out. Today, I want to turn around and start living my life on your road where your peace, joy, happiness, and success is. I want you to teach and show me the plans you have for me each day. And give me the patience I need to wait on your instruction and direction for my life. Amen." If you just prayed that prayer, congratulations! Jesus is going to show you great and mighty things when you travel on his road, I can assure you of that. All you have to do now is listen and follow Jesus' four steps in the last part of the book which will help keep you on the right road.

Key questions to ask yourself

• Do you know what road you're traveling on?

• Have you made a fork-in-the-road decision in your life?

• Are you living your life for the things of this world?

Key points to remember

• We can't live on Jesus' road and the Devil's at the same time.

• If any man loves this world the love of God is not in him.

• Only Jesus narrow road leads to a successful happy life.

God's promises to remember

• The eye has not seen, nor ear heard, nor have entered
into the heart of man, the things which God has prepared
for them who love him. (I Corinthians 2:9, NKJV)

• Blessed is everyone that fears the Lord, who walks
in his ways. When you eat of the labor of your hands.
You shall be happy, and it shall be well with you. (Psa. 128:1, 2)

• But he who does the will of God abides forever. (I John 2:17, NKJV)

CHAPTER 3

GOD HAS PLANS FOR
YOU TO BE SUCCESSFUL

I believe we need to have good success in all that we do first before we can truly be happy. In my research talking with people about success and happiness, I ask the question, "If you had to choose between the two, would you rather be successful or happy?" The answer I always get is they would rather be happy first. I believe the reason for that is people have a different definition of what success is as opposed to being happy. But before we talk further about it, we first need to define its true meaning.

In general success is determined by the end results of something that ends up being favorable or profitable to you. In other words, if you lost something valuable or important and found it later, you would call that success. If you baked a cake and it turned out exactly how you wanted it, that would be success. If you planned your wedding and everything turned out just the way you wanted it to, that would be success. In other words, no matter what it is we do or plan, we want the end results to be successful, a favorable outcome. The question is do we seek our own plans for success or do we seek God's? That's my goal, to help you find the answer to that question in this chapter and throughout the book. Because one thing I found that you won't see or hear being advertised anywhere is God's success program except for in the bible. And the only way you can find that out is through Jesus himself because he is success. Jesus is the one who will determine what true success is. He said, "**Look, I am coming soon! my reward is with me and I to give to each person according to what they have done.** *I am the Alpha and the omega, the first and the last, the beginning and the end.*" (Revelation 22:12, 13, NIV) In other words, Jesus is the one who is going to be handing out the success rewards. That's why we need to listen to him and follow his program if you want true success. He created you with a purpose and perfect plan that is specially designed for you. In fact, you were so important the bible says God planned your purpose on earth before the world even began. (II Timothy 1:9, KJV) It says, "Who hath saved us, and called us with a holy calling, not according to our works, but **according to his own purpose and grace, which was given us in Christ Jesus before the world began.**" That means your purpose on earth is more important to God than anything else He created in this world. Not only does He have a purpose for you, He has plans for your life also. The bible says, "*For I know the plans I have for you, declares the Lord, plans to prosper you and not harm you, plans to give you hope and a future.*" (Jeremiah 29:11, NIV) Notice God didn't say, "I have plans for you to be happy"; he said his plans are for us to be successful first. And when we listen and follow his plans, that's when we have favorable outcomes called success. And the more favorable outcomes you have in your life, the happier you're going to be. The only thing you have to do on your part is follow his plan instead of yours; that's the key which we'll talk more about later. The only way we can mess that up is by not trusting God and making our own plans for success as King Saul did. True success only comes from God, not from our own goals and achievements. When we set out to seek our own plans and goals for success outside of God's will, we're wasting our time. On the other hand, when you do his will and follow His plan, He guarantees success because He's behind it. For example, as much as possible I like to buy products or services that have a 100 percent satisfaction guaranteed or your money back. Because if you're not satisfied with the outcome, you can get your money back. In other words, you can't lose when the maker of the product takes the risk factor out. But it still doesn't guarantee you're going to have successful results to your satisfaction. The truth is God is the only one who can guarantee 100 percent successful results every single time. Because he's the one who ultimately determines the outcome of everything. On the other hand, man can't do that but he sure likes to try. My point is God is the only one who can truly guarantee success in your life without a risk factor. —as long as you follow His plans like He did with Noah, Abraham, Joseph, Moses, Joshua, David and many others. I have learned that when you follow God's plans for success, it always has a favorable outcome. Jesus said, "I am the beginning and the end"; that means everything he created is already planned out and determined with a successful end, most importantly your life.

What kind of foundation are you building your life on?

God made us all with a purpose and a plan for his own pleasure to enjoy. For example, if you wanted to build yourself a perfect dream house, would you just hire a bunch of contractors and tell them to start building a house without any plans first? Of course not; the first thing you do is start out with a vision of what you want it to look like. That's why you call it a dream house because you thought of it and created it to please yourself. The next thing you do is put your vision on paper called a blueprint. Once you have the blueprint, the next thing is a plan with steps. The first and most important step is the foundation—because if you don't get the foundation right, then everything you build on top of it isn't going to last the test of time. That is the same principle Jesus warns us about in our lives when he tells the story about the two foundations and two kinds of men in Matthew 7:24–27. Jesus says whoever listens to me and does it will be a successful wise man who built his house on a rock. The rock is the foundation of Jesus Christ who is your salvation. And whatever you build upon him such as your marriage and your plans for your life is all going to have success and last forever. Jesus says there are two kinds of men:

the man who built his house upon a rock and the other man who built his house on the sand. And they both had the same set of problems when the rain, floods, and wind blew and beat upon both their houses. And when the storm was over, the wise man was successful because he built his house on the rock which was still standing. On the other hand, the foolish man was unsuccessful because he chose to build his house on the sand that had no real foundation and he lost everything he built. In other words, Jesus is saying if you want to live a successful life on earth, then you need to build your life on him. Keep in mind he said you're going to have the same storms in your life as the foolish man. The only difference is you're going to last through it all and keep everything you built on him like with Noah. The point to learn from this parable is that Jesus gives two choices but only one is successful. The question that matters most is which one of the foundations are you building your marriage, family, business, and the plans of your life on—the rock (Jesus Christ) or the sand of this world? This world is full of stories of people who built their life on the sand; everything seems to start out just perfect and everyone's happy. Then comes the storms of this life and it's all washed away, even the foundation. I know that personally: it happened to me when I built my first business. It grew fast. I was having good success. It looked like I was successful from the outside. Then one day the storms of the recession came on top of my foolish way of living. The next thing I know my business plans and dreams are all washed away. I thank God that in the beginning me and my wife made the decision to build our marriage, family, and house on the rock Jesus Christ. Because that was the only thing that was left standing and still is today. After the loss of my first business and doing things my way, I couldn't afford for that to happen again. That's when I decided to build everything in my life on the foundation of Jesus Christ. Because it's all guaranteed to be successful and last the test of time on earth and through eternity. The best part is I don't worry about what the storms of this life can bring anymore. Because everything I do now is built on him and by him that's where the peace and security comes in.

The next steps after the foundation are the basement, the floor, the walls, the roof and siding.

After that, you can start on the inside down to all the finishing work. And if everything goes well and is finished on time and according to your plans, you would call that a successful outcome. It wasn't a coincidence that it ended that way: it was by your design and plan from beginning to end. That is the same kind of success situation that God has for your life. As long as you stick to His plans, you're going to have a successful outcome in everything you do. On the other hand, if you choose your own plans instead of God's, that's when we experience unsuccessful results. That's because He is the master builder with the plans, not us. The bible says, "*Unless the Lord builds the house, they labor in vain that build it.*" (Psalms 127:1, NKJV)

That statement can't be said any bolder than that. In other words, we're wasting our time trying to build our life according to our plans and expecting everything to work out. How would you like it if every time you showed up on the job site, you see your contractors not following your plans like you specified? How would that make you feel? What would you do? Probably fire them right away and replace them with someone who will carry out your plans. You don't have time for that: you have a deadline to meet. On the other hand, God has His purpose, plan, and deadline to meet for your life. The questions is are you holding him up with yours? Thank God for His patience and grace when we don't stick to His plans that he doesn't always replace us right off the bat.

God created us with a purpose to glorify Him

God made you a one-of-a-kind masterpiece with a master plan. Fully equipped with the necessary abilities and talent for you to be successful to glorify Him with. He says, "*Everyone who is called by my name, for I have created him for my glory. I have formed him, yea, I have made him.*" (Isaiah 43:7, KJV) Notice that God says everyone is created for his glory, no special person group or race. That's what I love about God.

Everyone has been specially equipped to glorify God and without any excuses of not having the ability to do so. Maybe you're someone who feels like your life was a mistake or your life doesn't really matter. If that's you, the good news is you don't have to feel that way anymore because God said everyone was created for His glory. That means you. When you believe you don't have any purpose, then there is no real meaning to life. That's exactly how the Devil wants you to think and believe and that's a big lie. Don't forget the Devil was created for God's glory too, until the day he wanted to steal it for himself. Just make sure you don't allow him to steal away your purpose and God's plans for you. God said we were planned for His purpose before the world even began; that would make it impossible for anyone to be a procreated mistake without a purpose. Nothing happens in this world without God's approval, permission, or him knowing about it, period. Another way to look at it is man never creates anything without a purpose in mind first, just like God, whether it's a fork to eat with, a shovel to dig a hole, or a rocket to go to the moon. Just look around you right now: everything you can see has its own purpose whether it's created by God or man. For anyone to believe they are some mistake or has no real purpose simply makes no sense when everything else in this world has. If that were true, that would make you the only person in the world who was created without a purpose or plan and that's ridiculous. Man always creates things for success just like God; the only difference is that God does it right the first time and doesn't make mistakes—whereas man makes mistakes until he gets it right and then he calls it success. It's been said Thomas Edison failed 1,000 times before he was successful inventing the first lightbulb. On the other hand, God was successful creating you for the right purpose the first time. You are a one-of-kind, preplanned success story created by Almighty God for His purpose, pleasure, and glory. One thing God doesn't do is make carbon copies of anything: no two things he creates are the exact same. Things may appear to look the same to us like a zebra or leopard, for example. The fact is there are no two zebras that have the same exact stripes or leopards that has the same exact spots. And there are no two people with the same exact purpose, plan, and success story. You are the only one who can do that. You may be saying, "Okay, how do I know what God's purpose and plan is for me?" Good question. I think that might be most people's; that was mine and still is.

Years ago I read a book called *Purpose-Driven Life* written by Rick Warren. If you haven't read it, I would encourage you do so. I read that at least five times because it helped me realize I wasn't born a mistake and I was created for a purpose to glorify God. And it was up to me to find out what that purpose and plan is and I will be doing that the rest of my life. I can't tell you what your specific purpose is or what God's plan is or can anyone else—only God knows that. Here's what I can help you with, showing you how to find that out for yourself step by step and day by day in the last chapters of this book.

God has shown me there are four steps, which I call His priorities, to finding true success and happiness. The four steps will help you find what His purpose and plan is for your life. I have learned that God doesn't show you His purpose and plans all at once: it may take your whole life-time to know that. He tells us to trust and follow his plans each day just like building the house one step and phase at a time: it doesn't happen overnight. You find that out as you go through life on a day-to-day basis. The main thing is listen to God and follow his plans and you will get there just like Joseph did. Before I knew God had a purpose and plan for my life to be successful, I felt pressured and unhappy. That's because I didn't know God had a purpose and daily plan for my life. I thought it was up to me to figure that out. Now I live a happy unpressured life knowing that God has a purpose and plans for me to be successful. The bottom line is do you want guaranteed success in your life? Then follow God's plan and you will achieve it without the stress, worry, or pressure the world gives. I have a little plaque in my office. It says, "You become successful the moment you start moving toward a worthwhile goal." God tells us there's no higher goal of success to move toward than seeking the purpose and will He has for your life.

The world's formula for success is total opposite of God's

The world measures success by fame, wealth, power, and self-achievements. The world tells you to be first and believe in yourself, follow your dreams, work hard, and accomplish your goals then you'll be successful. I'm not saying that's not a formula for success because it is according to the world's standards it's just not God's. Nowhere in the bible does God ever tell us to follow our dreams, work hard and make your own plans, and trust in ourselves for success. In fact God says just the opposite. He says, "Cursed be the man that trust in man." I would encourage you to read the rest of that in (Jeremiah 17:5–11, KJV) In other words, the best policy is to put all your trust in God. Why? He's never going to cheat you or let you down, and you can always count on him 100 percent of the time. David in my opinion was the most successful person in the bible and one of his most frequent quotes is "Happy is the man that puts his trust in God first." God tells us to follow Jesus not ourselves or our dreams. Jesus said, "*I am the way, the truth, and the life.*" (John 14:6, KJV) God never tells us we need to work hard to be successful like the world says to do. Right from the beginning God never intended for us to work hard at all. That was our curse and punishment. He wants to help make our work easier because if we're working hard and under stress all the time, it makes it difficult to enjoy his presence and enjoy life. Jesus doesn't tell us to work hard while you're young, save for retirement then rest and enjoy yourself like the world tells us. He says we can have it right now if we learn to walk with him and learn his ways. And his way for success is making your goal to do his will by accomplishing his plans he already has for you. And whatever prosperity and success God gives us, he expects the credit for it. The bible says, "*Therefore, whether you eat, or drink, or **whatever you do, do all to the glory of God.**" (I Corinthians 10:31, NKJV) My favorite success stories in the bible that have helped me the most are about Joseph, Joshua, and David. I studied their lives because of their success from the beginning to end. God was the common denominator. He was the reason for all their success and not anything they did themselves. They all followed the same principles which I call God's success in a nutshell. They always put God first; they put their trust in his plans, they were committed and carried them out, and they always gave him the glory. Listen to what God told Joshua, *"Keep this book of the law always on your lips; meditate on it day and night, so that you may be careful to do everything written in it,* ***then you will be prosperous and successful.*** (Joshua 1:8, NIV)

David said, *"Blessed is the man who walks not in the counsel of the ungodly, nor stands in the path of sinners, nor sits in the seat of the scornful. But his delight is in the law of the Lord; and in his law he meditates day and night. He shall be like a tree planted by the rivers of water, that brings forth its fruit in his season; whose leaf also shall not wither;* ***and whatsoever he does shall prosper.*** (Psalms 1:1–3, NKJV) Remember when claiming God's promises he always requires us to do something first before you get the benefit of the promise. In other words, God told Joshua he had to do three things before he would promise good success. He had to keep his word, think about him all the time, and do all the things he asked. I remember when I first read those promises years ago I thought that was a lot of hoops to jump through for God's success. Especially the part thinking about him all the time—I didn't understand that till years later in my life. You might be saying the same thing, "How in the world can I think about God all day and all night? I have a very busy schedule and have too many distractions in my life to think about God all the time. My job requires my thinking every minute and then I come home to my family and kids who need my immediate attention. Then I have chores to do and if I'm lucky I might have a few minutes left for myself—and I have to try to think about God during all that?" Absolutely 100 percent yes, that used to be me. I have since learned it's not hard at all when you have your priorities right. It comes down to this: you have your set of priorities and God has His. The question is whose are you going to do first? God has the power to make our life successful and a lot easier if we put him first in all that we do. Remember Jesus said, "Walk with me not run," and "Learn from me. My ways are easy. That's when you will find rest unto your soul." Jesus isn't talking about a good night's sleep here;

he's talking about finding rest in your soul even while you're busy. When you're thinking about God, He's thinking about you; that's how you enjoy His presence. It's not a hard thing to think about something all the time; as long as it's something you love, then it's a priority.

For example, I remember when I first fell in love with my wife. When we were first dating, I was so infatuated with her that all I did was think about her from morning till night. I would think about her while I was working, watching the clock waiting for my shift to end just so I could go see her. When you love someone or something, that's all you can think about. It consumes you no matter how busy you are. God wants us to think about Him in the same way. You don't have to stop what you're doing. The only time I used to think about God was when I needed something—prayed before a meal or at church. And if that's you, you're missing out big time, especially all of God's benefits with the joy of his presence. That's why David praised Him seven times a day and couldn't wait to start talking with Him first thing before the sun came up. David couldn't wait to see what God had planned for him the next day. We should be excited in that same way. When you're following God's plan, there should not be one day that goes by in your life that you don't see His favor or hand helping you in some way.

God wants to be your helper

God knows all about your day and how it's going to unfold before it even begins. And each day we live in is going to be filled with problems, troubles, and situations. And he wants to help you with all of them no matter how big or small they are. Most of the time it's just small problems we deal with on a daily basis. Years ago I thought God was only there to help me on big problems in my life, like when my wife had her brain tumor and we needed a miracle. I never bothered to ask him for help with small problems. I just dealt with that stuff myself. Boy, did I miss out!

I have since learned God wants to help you with everything right down to the finest detail. If you want to have successful outcomes in every aspect of your life, then ask God for his help and wisdom. David said, "All of my help comes from the Lord who made heaven and earth," that's why he was so successful. David was hated by his enemies and his own king because of one reason: they were jealous of all his successes and God being his helper. And no matter how hard they tried to kill him, they were never successful because God was his shield and helper. God said, "*The enemy shall not outwit him, or the son of wickedness afflict him.*" (Psalms 89:22, NKJV) If you know David's story from the time of his youth till the day he died, he always gave God the credit. In fact, he even died successfully; in other words, he lived to be a good old age, got to see his son take over his throne, and died a peaceful death. And on his deathbed his last words were instructions to his son Solomon on how to have the same success he had. He told him, "If you walk in God's ways and keep his commandments whatsoever you do you will prosper and have good success. And no matter who you are if you follow the same instructions, you're going to have good success in your life too. God not only wants to be your helper but he also wants to show you his favor and goodness. God says, "*For those who find me find life and receive favor from the Lord.* (Proverbs 8:35, NIV)

The key to receiving God's favor is you have to find him first. In other words, be tuned into his presence by thinking about him and that he is always there ready to help. Some days you may not have any problems which is rare, but you always can use God's favor in some situation. Like finding the right job, getting promoted, or getting the best deal on something like a house, a car, or anything you need. I have found it can be as simple as someone letting you have cuts in line at the grocery store when you need it most. Or the parking lot is full and you need a spot to park in. It happens to me all the time when we go boating. For example, the place I see God's favor the most is at our lake's boat launch parking lot. It's a beautiful lake that has become very popular, so the parking spots get filled up early usually by noon on a weekend and can stay full for 2–3 hours. I don't like to get there that early just to get a parking spot and we live less than a mile away. I could always drive the boat trailer back to our house but that's a bit of a hassle. It makes life a lot easier to have a parking spot. By the time I want to go is the busiest time and the parking lot is always full. When I pull in, I ask the attendant how long it has been full. He usually says, "A couple of hours." Then my wife says, "What are we going to do?" I tell her the same thing all the time: we wait for God's favor to show up. So far his favor has always showed up, meaning someone's getting off the lake, giving us a parking spot. I haven't had to wait more than 15 minutes or drive the trailer back yet.

The next time you are in a situation where you could use God's favor, ask him for it. If you start practicing that, you'd be surprised at how many times you will see his favor show up. The more you're aware of God, the more of his favor you'll see. And there are times when he shows you his favor before you can even think to ask. Every time that happens I think that's the coolest thing in the world, because you know he was behind it. On the other hand, there can be times when you need God's help and favor immediately. I needed that this summer. We were on our way up north to go camping and boating pulling our boat. It was hot and humid, about 95 degrees. We were about 100 miles from home and halfway to our destination. We're on the highway and the engine light came on, telling me to stop the engine. So I pulled over and the radiator was over-heating. It was the water pump going bad. I said, "Oh God, no! Please help me," I don't know how many times. I told my wife, "We are done. There's no vacation now." She said, "Don't panic." I said to myself, "God, why is this happening to me?" I prayed for a safe trip there and back. Yes, I was panicking while my wife was acting like there was some hope that we could still continue on our vacation. I said, "How in the world are we going to get this fixed and still go on vacation unless God does some kind of miracle?" We are like 20 miles from any main city. It's the weekend, 95 degrees out with an engine ready to burn up pulling a boat on top of it. While I was waiting for the engine to cool back down, I told my wife I'd like to see how God helps us out of this one and still go on vacation. I remembered what David said when he was in trouble in Psalms 102:1–2. I found myself saying the same thing. I said, "Oh Lord, I am in trouble. I need your help right now. Please answer me quickly. Tell me what I need to do." I could see we were about 1 mile away from the next exit. Once the engine cooled down, I took the risk of driving to it to the exit and see if I could get help. There was a store, so I pulled in to the parking lot to find some water. There was a woman who saw me with my hood up and said, "Are you having trouble?" I said yes and asked her if she knew of any auto mechanic garages nearby. She told me there were two, both close to each other 1 mile away. And that was all the farther I could drive without losing all the water and risk burning up the engine. The first place was all booked up and couldn't help us because it was a Friday afternoon. Our last hope was the second place, otherwise we would have to get our vehicle and boat towed all the way back home. I called the guy, told him my problem, and asked if he could help me today. He said, "Yes, come on in." When he said that, I could not believe it. That was the best yes I have ever heard. When I got there, I saw it was a small auto garage way off the beaten path. You would never know it was there unless somebody told you, which that woman did. When I walked in, I thought to myself, "What is the chance they even have the right part?" There was someone waiting before me and I heard the guy at the desk tell him he wouldn't be able to fix his vehicle until Monday, which allowed me to get right in.

They had the right part. Then I asked him how long it will take to put the new pump in. He said about 2 ½ hours. I could not believe this was even happening. One minute I was stranded on the highway 95 degrees out, no help in sight. It all seemed hopeless as far as staying on schedule to make it to our vacation destination. The next thing I know I was sitting in air condition watching TV waiting for our vehicle to get fixed which only took 2 hours. The total time we lost from the time of breakdown to successfully being back on the road again was 3 hours. I couldn't believe it. I thought for sure we were going to be towed back home. Instead, it ended up being one of the best summer vacations we've had, including our breakdown. I told my wife even if that same situation happened right in our own driveway, we'd have to be towed. And I don't believe we could have gotten that fixed in 3 hours and be on the road again. I won't ever forget that situation. God listened to my cry and helped me speedily. He had me break down at the right spot with the right people to help me. The lesson I learned from that is don't try to figure out how God is going to help you when you can't see any way. Just cry unto him and ask for his help quickly and watch how the hand of God works helping you out of all your troubles. God is thinking about you and watching over you 24/7. The question is are you thinking about him? God already knows the problems and situations you're going to face each day and he has the solution to every single one of them. David had more trouble and problems in his life than any one I have ever read about. David said, "**For he hath delivered me out of all my troubles.** (Psalms 54:7, KJV) He didn't say some of his troubles: he said all of his troubles. When I read that for the first time, I couldn't believe it. That's a pretty bold statement. I thought, "How could anyone be helped out of all their troubles? To me that is a perfect problem-solving record. That is the verse that caused me to start studying David's life, to find out if that was really true or not. I could not find anywhere in David's life that God did not help him out of all his troubles in some way and not even the ones he caused himself. That caused me to think about my own life's troubles; unlike David, most of those I caused myself. I couldn't think of any trouble I had in my life that God did not help me out in some way. Oh, I had to pay the consequence bill for the sin trouble I caused myself. But by God's grace, mercy, and pity on my soul, he has helped me out of every single one of them too. That's one thing I have a hard time understanding, how much of God's grace and mercy He has shown towards me for all my foolishness. The only thing that makes any sense to me is God said He chooses to use the foolish things of this world to confuse the wise. I believe God allows problems and troubles in our life so we will rely on Him for his help. That's why we need to always be aware of His presence because he truly is our helper.

True success will be determined at the judgment seat of Christ

The only success that is going to matter to God in the end is how well we followed his will for our life. The bible says one day we all are going to give an account of what we did with our time, money, and talents He gave us. The question to ask yourselves: are you using them for your own purposes or for His kingdom and glory? That question is going to be answered one day by Jesus which is called the judgment seat of Christ. He will be the ultimate test of what true success is. Christians aren't going to be judged for their sins that day; that's already a done deal paid for by Jesus' blood on the cross. In other words, if you have already accepted Jesus Christ as your personal savior, you have your ticket into heaven. Salvation is a free gift from God. You don't have to work for that. But there's more to it than that: you do have to work for your rewards, and you do have to give an account of your time, money, and talent: how you spent them here on earth. I don't think a lot of Christians even know about the Judgment seat of Christ. Because that's one subject you just don't hear much about anymore, which I don't fully understand. In fact, in all my years of going to church, I never heard that subject talked about once. Except by Jack Van Impe himself, a TV evangelist I heard over forty years ago. That stuck in my mind and I never forgot it. If everybody likes receiving a reward, then why shouldn't we be talking more about the awards ceremony for Christians, especially when it will last through all eternity? The bible says, *"We must all appear before the judgment seat of Christ, that everyone may receive the things done in his body according to that he has done whether it be good or bad."* (II Corinthians 5:10, KJV) In other words, God is warning us ahead of time there is going to be a day that true success will be revealed and that success will be tested by fire. The apostle Paul tells us true success that will last into eternity can only be built on the foundation of Jesus Christ: any other way will not last. *For no other foundation can anyone lay than that which is laid which is Jesus Christ. Now if any man builds on this foundation with gold, silver, precious stones, wood, hay, straw, each one's work will become clear, for the day will declare it. Because it will be revealed by fire; and the fire will test each one's work, of what sort it is. If anyone's work which he has built on it endures, he will receive a reward. If anyone's work is burned, he will suffer loss, but he himself will be saved yet so as through fire.* (I Corinthians 3:11–15, NKJV)

In other words, there is going to be two kinds of categories of what you did with your time, money, and talent here on earth. The first one is the success category which will be the gold, silver, and precious stones which represents your time, money, and talent you invested in Jesus and his kingdom. The second one is the unsuccessful category called the wood hay and stubble which represents your time, money, and talent you invested in this world for your own purposes other than Jesus' kingdom. The wood hay and stubble can't make it through the fire test without getting burned up. That believer is going to suffer loss because he has nothing to go into eternity with except for his soul, which shall be saved by fire. In other words, there's going to be some believers in heaven who are saved by the skin of their teeth. I don't know how you feel when you read that. For me, I don't like the thought of suffering any kind of loss period, much less for eternity. Our only chance to change that is what we do here and now on earth for Jesus that determines our success in eternity. God isn't going to care about your wealth status or how famous you were or about your personnel accomplishments. When you appear before the almighty God, the bible makes it perfectly clear He's only going to care about one thing: how well you carried out His will with your time, money, and talent for His glory and His kingdom. If you're a Christian, Jesus has already warned us now is the time to start preparing yourself for eternity. You do that by getting rid of any wood hay and stubble you have in your life and replace it with gold, silver, and precious stones. For example, I used to be an amateur boxer when I was young and old. In my office on my wall, I have boxing trophies, newspaper articles, and other tokens of achievements. One of my biggest accomplishments in boxing was when I turned forty-one years old. I decided to go back out for the golden gloves and my goal was to be the oldest amateur in history to ever win a state championship. The boxing board would not let me fight, said I was too old. The age limit was thirty-two. So I wrote a letter, told them I would file a lawsuit for age discrimination. They finally backed down and told me I would have to go through all kinds of extensive physical exams and tests first to be deemed fit to compete because of my age. I passed all the tests. The news media heard about it. They interviewed me, wrote the story, and put it on the front sports page. That for me was an accomplishment just to be on the front of the sports page. That's because in amateur boxing, forty-one years old is unheard of, especially fighting kids half your age. The truth is I wanted to be in the limelight. I wanted that feeling of winning the championship again and making history on top of it. I wanted that trophy, all the glory and recognition that goes along with it. That's what I like most about the sport of boxing: the winner gets all the glory and doesn't have to share it with anyone. If that sounds selfish, it's true. It even sounds a lot like how Satan wanted all the glory for himself. Back then I wasn't looking at it the way as I do now. I ended up winning the West Michigan championship and was runner-up in the state championship. My point here as I look back on it all now is that the hard work and time I put in for that kind of success was for the wrong reasons. The trophies, the glory, the recognition, and 15 minutes of fame are all going to be worthless wood hay stubble and burned up one day. Because I did it all for myself and my glory and not God's. I thank God He has given me the chance and wisdom showing me what true success is really all about. In other words, if you want to be truly successful at something that's going to last through all eternity, set a goal to accomplish God's will for your life whatever that is and do it all for his glory. Jesus warns us, "**Lay not up for yourselves treasure upon earth,** *where moth and rust does corrupt, and where thieves break through and steal,* **But lay up for yourselves treasures in heaven** *where neither moth nor rust does corrupt, and where thieves do not break through nor steal:* **for where your treasure is, there will your heart be also.**" (Matthew 6:19–21, KJV) He warns us again: "**Do not love the world or the things in this world. If anyone loves the world, the love of the father is not in him.** *For all that is in the world the lust of the flesh, the lust of the eyes, and the pride of life is not of the father but is of the world.* **And the world is passing away, and the lust of it, but he who does the will of God abides forever.**" (I John 2:15–17, NKJV) In other words, Jesus is telling us how to be successful on earth and in heaven. In a nutshell, it's about doing all the things that are in God's will. How can you go wrong doing what he wants you to do? According to his word you can't; that is the key to true success, doing his will not ours. For example, suppose God were to allow you to live up to eighty to ninety years and you spent those years building your kingdom for yourself and the things of this world. When it was your turn at the rewards ceremony, the judgment seat of Christ, you see all the things you worked hard for on earth burned up in a flash. Could you spend the rest of eternity thinking about that? Would it be worth it? What's eighty to ninety years compared to eternity? That's why Jesus is warning us, saying, "What does it profit a man if he gain the whole world and in the end he either loses his soul or suffers loss?" I don't know how any reasonable person could think that would be a profitable deal. Yet I believe the majority of Christians are living their lives that way every day. The apostle Paul says, "The things that I used to think to be profitable for me I now count as loss for Christ." All the things he could have done he now counts as dung. In other words, a worthless waste in comparison to the things that are done for Christ that will last for eternity. The bottom line is Jesus is the one who determines true success both on earth and in heaven. Are you prepared for the judgment seat of Christ? Which one of the believers do you want to be? Jesus is not only our Lord and Savior, he is also our accountant (Romans 14:12), judge (Romans 14:10), and rewarder (Revelation 22:12). We have no excuses why we can't be successful, because Jesus is the true definition of success. He came here and set the example and made it perfectly clear how to be successful with our time, money, and talents. I can think of no higher honor of success than to hear Jesus say one day, "Well done, good and faithful servant," as he's handing out your rewards. In my opinion, just hearing Jesus say those words alone with a big hug would be better than winning any championship reward for me. I feel like I have already gotten my reward with all the chances he has given me on earth with his grace and mercy. That's my number one goal and I put it in my daily prayer by saying, "Lord, show me how to live my life each day to where you will say to me one day, 'Well done, good and faithful servant.'" If I can't hear those words, then nothing else matters. According to Jesus, that's the highest recognition you can get. Here's what I learned and like about Jesus' success program. First of all, it's the only true success rewards program there is that will last through eternity. Your time, money, and talent that you invest into Jesus' kingdom is 100 percent guaranteed to never depreciate for all eternity. That's because it's backed by God's word and not a bank. No one can make that promise other than Jesus himself. In other words, in his investment program you don't have to worry about what the stock markets are doing. Jesus promises your investment profits will never get eaten up, lose its value, or get stolen. Now do you know of any investment program that can top that? I know I haven't found one. If you want guaranteed success, start investing into Jesus' eternity rewards program. Remember Jesus' last words were, "Behold everybody listen up! I'm going to come quicker than you think in your life. In other words, be ready! Because I have my rewards I'm going to be giving to every man according to what he did on earth with his time, money, and talent for my kingdom. I am the beginning and the end, the first and the last. Blessed and successful you will be if you do my commandments." (Revelation 22:12–14)

Questions to ask yourself

- What kind of foundation are you building your life on?

- Are you following your dreams or God's will for a successful life?

- Are you investing into Jesus rewards program?

Key points to remember

- Unless the Lord builds the house, they who build it labor in vain.

- The worlds view of success is the enemy of God.

- The judgment seat of Christ will determine what true success is.

God's promises

• For I know the plans I have for you, declares the Lord,
Plans to prosper and not to harm you, plans to
Give you hope and a future. (Jeremiah 29:11, NIV)

• Who hath saved us, and called us with a holy calling,
Not according to our works, but according to his own
purpose and grace, which was given us in Christ Jesus
before the world began. (II Timothy 1:9, KJV)

• For those who find me find life and receive favor
from the Lord. (Proverbs 8:35, NIV)

CHAPTER 4

TRUE HAPPINESS CAN ONLY BE FOUND IN GOD

Happiness is one thing that every one of us wants, one that we can't live without. Every day from the time we wake up to the time we go to bed, our subconscious' actions are motivated by seeking happiness. We all want to make ourselves feel happy or satisfied one way or another. It's our human nature to pursue after it because that's the way God created us. In fact, we are so consumed about being happy that if anyone or anything tries to prevent or keep us from it, we would eliminate the problem by any means necessary, even to the extreme of killing over it. The freedom to pursue happiness is the main principle the United States of America was founded on. In our declaration of Independence our founding fathers said, "We hold these truths to be self-evident that all men are created equal, that they are endowed by their Creator (God) with certain unalienable rights, and among these are Life, Liberty, and the pursuit of Happiness. It's no accident the United States of America is the most successful and prosperous country in the world It's because our founding fathers had their priorities in the right order. In other words, they put God first when they said all men are created equal with the right to live and have the freedom to pursue happiness. And let us not forget our country was founded on God's word and God-fearing men and women who put him first. They trusted in God's help to win the battles needed to be able to obtain the freedoms we now have to pursue happiness. They not only trusted God but they also gave him the credit for their victories and successes. If you look at our military history, most of the battles we should have never won. Because God was on our side, He gave us the victories and successes that we needed to obtain our freedoms we have today. Let us never forget God and all the souls of men and women who sacrificed their lives for the freedoms we have today to pursue happiness. I believe our forefathers knew what could happen if we ever did forget God. That's why we have "In God we trust" on our money, in our national anthem, and in our pledge of allegiance to remind us that we are one nation under God. Our schools at one time opened up with prayer that went something like "Almighty God, we acknowledge our dependence on Thee and give your blessing over us, our parents, our teachers, and our nation." Until 1962, when the courts ruled that official prayer had no place in public education. Since that ruling in 1962, school crime has increased by over 800 percent. I personally believe that decision has contributed in part to the crime problems we have in our schools today. I say that because anytime you remove God from anything, that's the biggest mistake you can ever make. Because when you remove God, eventually over a period of time you will forget him. And the last thing in the world you want to do is forget God. Not only as a country: it starts with you your family, your town, city, state—and that's what your country becomes. All I'm saying is when we forget God, we are asking for trouble instead of peace, joy, and happiness. History speaks for itself. Look what happened in the days of Noah, Sodom and Gomora when people forget God. That's why we need to daily remind ourselves it is God who allows us the freedom to pursue happiness in this great country we are so blessed to live in. King David warns us what will happen if we forget God. He says, *"The wicked shall be turned into hell **and all nations that forget God**.* (Psalms 9:17, KJV) It doesn't get any bolder or straightforward than that.

Thank God our congress still opens in prayer every day. Someone must have believed what David had to say. Our congress knows they have a world full of problems they have to deal with every day and they need all of God's help and blessings they can get. The purpose of prayer is not just to ask God for things and his blessings, but to first thank him for all the things he has already blessed us with and the freedom to enjoy it. Because without freedom, you can't really enjoy life and God's goodness. Freedom and happiness are at the core of existing at all. What's the point of living if you don't have the freedom to enjoy happiness? Remember what our forefathers said: "Give me freedom or give me death." That should be a daily reminder and at the top of our prayer list. Without God's help and our military, we would not have the freedom we have today to pursue happiness. So help us God that we never take for granted the freedom and prosperity God has already blessed us with. David said, "Be happy in the Lord all you righteous and give thanks and remember he is God." If you're a veteran or in the military, I want you to know you are always in my prayers. I thank God every day for the sacrifice of your time and for all those who gave the ultimate sacrifice: their lives. Jesus said there is no greater love than a man who is willing to lay down his life for his friends. And for those of us who have never served in the military, let us pray for those who have and not forget their sacrifices and take our freedom for granted. David said blessed is the nation whose God is the Lord. It's not a coincidence this is the greatest country in the world. I believe it's because it was founded on God's word and principles that's why we have the largest population of Christians in the world at over 80 percent. When a person or people put their trust in God and stand for godly principles, then make no mistake about it, God is on their side. David proved that time and time again especially with Goliath. He said, "When God is on my side, I will not fear what man can do unto me." Our country has proved that time and time again with victory over or adversaries. If you want victory in your life, make sure God is on your side.

When we seek happiness outside of God's approval

It's one thing to have the freedom to pursue what you may think is happiness and it's another thing to find true happiness. You're probably saying what is true happiness by now. The difference is true happiness can only come from God just like all things true and good come from God. On the other hand, the Devil tries to sell us on his happiness. Don't forget he's a master at disguising the things of God.

To understand this more, we first have to realize that God created us with a void or emptiness in our soul for happiness. He created us that way so we can only truly be satisfied and happy with his presence instead of what you may think will make you happy. David said, "*In your presence is the fullness of joy*. (Psalms 16:11, NKJV) That is, the key to true happiness is God's presence in whatever it is you're doing, as long as it is approved by him. He created us to have a loving happy relationship with him during our time on earth. When you love someone, you want to be with them and enjoy things together and be happy, right? That's exactly what God wants to do with us. He wants to be part of everything that we do, especially being happy. The problem comes when we try to seek happiness outside of his approval limits or commandments. And when we do that, there is always a consequence we have to pay for called sin. God's not going to approve sin just so we can be happy our way. That's never going to happen. Adam and Eve didn't get away with it and neither would we. In other words, if God can't be part of what you're doing, then his presence won't be there. And if his presence is not there, then you're robbing yourself of the true happiness that only God can give. A perfect example of that is the life of King Solomon, the wisest, richest man to ever live. The bible said he tried everything under the sun to make himself happy and still couldn't find it. After years of studying his life, I believe I finally figured out why. He tried to find happiness in everything under the sun except for the presence of God himself. He spent his whole life trying to pursue one thing, happiness, and never found it. And I still don't understand how, with all his wisdom, he missed that when the answer was there all the time. The reason he couldn't find true happiness is he was looking for it in everything under the sun instead of above it, God himself. I think when God gave him all that wisdom, riches, and power, he may have felt like he was God. Think about it: all he had to do was ask God like he did for wisdom. "God, show me the thing that truly makes a man happy but he never did". Instead, he took it upon himself to find it out because he had all the means in the world to do it. Put yourself in his shoes: if God let you be the wisest, richest, most powerful person in the world, would you think to ask God that question or would you try to find that out yourself? I know I wouldn't have before God revealed to me what true happiness really is. The lesson for us to learn from his story is the answer: God's presence. David his father knew that and found it. As to whether he told that to his son, we will never know. But all that matters right now is you finding it. The best way I can explain it is God created us all with what I call a happiness tank. It is only reserved for him (his presence, joy, and happiness), but we try to fill it with everything without him or his approval like Solomon did with all his women. That would be like you trying to fill your car's gas tank with propane or anything else other than the right gas. If you try to use anything other than the right gas, it's not going to run, plus you'll damage the motor. That is no different from you trying to fill up your happiness tank with anything you think is going to make you happy. And if it's outside the limits of God's approval, there's always going to be a consequence that ends in unhappiness. It all started back with Adam and Eve and we still try to do it today. On the other hand, true happiness from God doesn't have any bad consequences because it has his approval. When we try to seek our own happiness outside of God's approval, we can never be fully satisfied. It reminds me of the time we get hungry and we eat to satisfy our hunger and then when we're full and satisfied, we're good for a little while till we get hungry again. The same is true with our happiness: when our happiness tank is low or empty, we seek to refill it again with something. Just like eating to satisfy our hunger, it never lasts; it's an ongoing cycle that will never change in our earthly bodies. Until we get to Heaven, that's when we will be completely satisfied and happy because we will be in the presence of God. That's the key here:

in the presence of God is true happiness. You don't have to wait to get to heaven for that. God gives us the choice to invite his presence into everything that we do here on earth. When we learn to do that, then we will be truly satisfied and happy. The bible says, *"The Lord shall guide thee continually and satisfy thy soul."* (Isaiah 58:11, KJV) In other words, he wants to be the one who continually satisfies our happiness tank. Notice he says "continually": that's because as I said earlier, it's an ongoing cycle and void that only God himself can fill. I believe he set it up that way so we will have to continually rely on him to fill our happiness tank like all the rest of our needs. On the other hand, you better be aware the Devil is going to be right there trying to sell you on his happiness gas. He's going to tell you that God's gas (his presence) is not the only thing that will make you happy. He's going to tell you how you can fill your happiness tank up with anything you want. And here's the part he always gets us with—you might want to highlight this, because it's the same old sales pitch he sold Adam and Eve on. The Devil reminds us that God has strict rules and limits because he doesn't want us to experience real happiness. That's the first big lie to get our attention to listen to his sales pitch. Then he tells us about all kinds of other ways we can make ourselves happy without God's approval and that's another lie. And the reason we fall for his lies is his ways actually sound better than God's; that's why he is the best salesman in the world. And here's that pitch he gets us all on: he tells us that happiness doesn't have rules or limits. You do what you want. On the other hand, God does have rules and limits to one's happiness.

The difference is His doesn't lead to destruction and chaos; it leads to peace, joy, and true happiness.

In other words, the Devil lies to us about happiness. I wasted a lot of good years before I figured that out. Plus I did not want God to be in charge of my happiness, because I knew that a lot of the things I was doing at the time was not approved by God. The Devil knew that too and I allowed him to take advantage of me and all of my weaknesses. The sad thing is a lot of people are doing the same thing, filling up their happy tank with the Devil's gas. And while they are doing it, they are damaging and destroying their lives. One of the most extreme measures people will take if they can't find happiness is committing suicide. In fact, the suicide rate is now at the highest it's ever been in this country's history, and over 75 percent are alcohol and drug related. People commit suicide for one main reason: they are not happy. They are so consumed about not being happy that the Devil and his demons gets them to believe they would be happier if they were dead. Then they don't have to spend each day thinking about why they are unhappy. The truth is the Devil doesn't want you to be happy and full of God's joy; he wants you to be sad, miserable, and dead if possible. God on the other hand wants you to live a happy, successful life. If you're a sad and miserable person right now, the first thing to do is stop listening to the Devil and his demons and start listening to God and claiming his promises. David said, "**Happy is that people whose God is the Lord.** (Psalms 144:15, KJV) God told Jeremiah, "*My people will be satisfied with my goodness, saith the Lord.*" (Jeremiah 31:14, KJV) On the other hand, Satan wants us to doubt God's goodness and he's always trying to convince us that we know what's best to make ourselves happy. The other extreme measure people will take if they can't find happiness is abusing alcohol and drugs like I did. As I'm writing this, my son and daughter are going to the memorial services of one of their friends—who had been slowly destroying herself with drugs for some time and last week finally overdosed and was found brain dead by her mother in her bedroom. After two days on life support, she died of a heart attack. She was only thirty-two years old, leaving behind her three children. Think about all the celebrities who have died from drug overdose, trying to find happiness: Elvis, Marilyn Monroe, John Belushi, Michael Jackson, Whitney Houston, and the list goes on. Most of us would think if we had their fame and money we would be happy, right? If that were true, then why take the risk of killing yourself? Truly happy people don't commit suicide or abuse themselves. When Elvis was at the pinnacle of his fame, he was asked this question from a reporter: "What is the one thing you'd like to have that you don't have now?" His answer was: "Happiness." He said, "You can have a big house nice car and all the things of this world and if you don't have happiness, then what do you have?" King Solomon said, "***Better is a little and the fear of the Lord than great treasure with trouble.*** (Proverbs 15:16, NKJV) If anyone has the experience to make that statement, he has. It's too bad he didn't live by his own words of wisdom, but that doesn't mean that we can't.

Bitterness and anger will destroy your happiness

I can speak from my own personal experience of abusing alcohol and drugs at the time. It was the only way I knew how to deal with my anger issues from my childhood. I was born an only child. My mother divorced my biological father when I was about one year old. She remarried when I was about two or three so I thought he was my real father. When I was about five years old, my mother explained to me that he wasn't my real father: he was my stepdad. I remember him as being a fun dad: he did all kinds of fun things with me. I remember being a happy kid until I was about eight years old and it all ended one day when he left my mother for another woman. That's when my happy world ended and about two years later when I was about ten, my mother remarried again, this time to a man who hated children. And that's all I needed to add to my already unhappy situation, a man who hated children. When she was dating him, she told me he didn't like children. One day she asked me how I felt about her marrying him. I remember it like it was yesterday: I told her if she married him, I would hate her for it. I was so angry I remember telling her that when I get married, I will never get divorced. She said, "You don't know what you're talking about. You're only ten years old." I think I meant that I've been happily married to my beautiful wife God gave me for forty-two years now. I went from having a happy world for about five years to an unhappy hated world, until I was eighteen when she divorced him. Although that was good news to me, it didn't much matter: it was too late. My childhood years were over. I lived with a stepfather who hated me for about ten years just because he didn't like kids in his way. Without realizing it, I had so much anger built up in me and I took it out on the rest of the world. I was in trouble all the time in school and out of school with the law. They didn't know what to do with me. From the time I was eleven years old, I started sniffing glue, lighter fluid, and from there marijuana, alcohol, acid, or any drug I could get my hands on just to escape the reality of being unhappy. That's all I wanted to do, be happy, and I thought I was happy when I was on drugs and alcohol. In reality all I was doing was numbing the pain of anger while destroying myself and getting in trouble. At seventeen years old my stepfather found marijuana in my room, called the police, and gave them permission to put me in jail back when it was illegal. Any opportunity he had to make my life miserable he'd do it. I abused drugs till I was eighteen years old. That's when I accepted Jesus Christ as my personal savior and started to put him first in my life. Thanks be to my beloved grandpa who always told me about Jesus and how he was always praying for me. Unfortunately, the anger I built up from my childhood has followed me most of my life, causing majority of my problems. I know there are a lot of people who have had a lot worse of childhood experience than mine. The only reason I'm telling you about mine is so you can see what God has done in my life to give hope and encouragement to others. I believe the majority of people are raised in some kind of dysfunctional way or another; some are just worse than the others that's all. The only *Leave It to Beaver* family I ever seen was on TV. The point I'm trying to make is we can't always control what others do to us, especially our parents. But we can control what we do to ourselves and others. That being said, it's not always easy to do, especially if you have years of built-up bitterness, resentment, and anger that doesn't just wash away. These in turn cause us to act out in dysfunctional behavior, such as abusing ourselves and others. If you were raised without a godly example to follow or in some kind of dysfunctional way, your only hope is in God. And as hard as it may be, the first thing you need to do is ask him to free you from any bitterness and anger you have. Without your forgiveness, it will eat you alive, destroying your happiness. Jesus said we need to forgive others if we want God to forgive us and to do unto others as we would want them to do to us. I wasted the first half my life doing just the opposite of what Jesus said. If anyone wronged me in any way, I took revenge and paid them back. If I couldn't pay you back, I had a special place reserved in my heart for you called the bitterness and anger department and you stayed there until you made it right with me. In the meantime, the problem with that is I was only hurting myself by walking around with stored up bitterness and anger just waiting to explode. That's like walking around with nitroglycerin in your pocket, knowing the second you get bumped it could explode, which makes you a dangerous person to be around. Jesus taught not to have any place in your heart reserved for unforgiven bitterness and anger. That's because Jesus wants us to be full of his joy and you can't be truly happy and have bitterness and anger at the same time. In James 3: 11, it says, "Does a fountain bring forth sweet water and bitter at the same place?" No, bitterness and anger will destroy your happiness just like bitter water destroys sweet water. The bible says, "Let all bitterness, wrath, anger and evil not have any place in you. Instead show kindness and forgive one another, even as God for Jesus sake has forgiven you." (Ephesians 4:31, 32) In other words, God doesn't want us to store up anger and wrath and unleash it for whom it is deserved. Remember God wants us to live happy and peaceful lives. He won't fill us with His Joy as long as we're full of anger and wrath. Don't worry about those who've wronged you; and don't think that just because you don't repay them back, they're getting away with it. The bible says, *"Do not take revenge, my dear friends but leave room for God's wrath; **its mine to revenge; I will repay says the Lord**. (Romans 12:17–21, NIV) In other words, put it in God's hands and let Him take care of the situation. He can do a lot better job than we can anyways. The bible says if it were all possible, we are to live peaceably with all men. Do you have any bitterness or anger issues in your life right now? If yes, the first thing to do if you want God's peace, joy, and happiness in your life is forgive others regardless of what they did. When we don't forgive, it does more damage to you than the other person. Because it does two things: one, it robs you of the happiness and joy that God has for you and two, your anger gives place to the Devil and his demons and things will just get worse from there. Trust me I've learned that the hard way. Replace that anger and bitterness with what Jesus said at the Sermon on the Mount Read (Matthew 5:3–12). Jesus taught the people there are nine ways to be happy and if you do those things, rejoice and be happy because you will have a great reward in heaven. Jesus said happy are the pure in heart. Happy are the peacemakers. Happy are those who show mercy. Happy are those who are persecuted for doing the right thing. Notice Jesus doesn't say happy are the angry or happy are those who hold resentment towards others and repay them back. Jesus tells us to do just the opposite, which is contrary to our natural nature which is why it's so difficult to do. When you have a forgiven heart, pursue peace, and show mercy to others, there is no room for bitterness and anger to destroy your happiness. One thing I learned is bitterness and anger is the demons' favorite food and when you get rid of it, they don't have anything to eat. They have to go find it somewhere else. I know this is a strange analogy but it gives you a visual image. If you rolled around in cow manure, I can guarantee you one thing: wherever you go, the flies are going to be all around and following you. On the other hand, the minute you wash yourselve off, the flies are going to be gone. Because there's nothing there to attract them. Hopefully you get my point. In other words, bitterness and unforgiveness attracts the Devil and his demons. Getting rid of bitterness and anger is what I did during rehab. It was one of the best decisions I ever made. I call it the turning point in my life. That's when I decided to let God turn my life around in the right direction by getting on the right road. By the time I entered rehab, I had so much bitterness and anger built up in me I was like a volcano constantly erupting. But this should give you some idea what my attitude was like then. After my second DUI, I was assigned a probation officer who told me I needed to go to rehab for thirty days. I told her she was out of her mind and I was not going. She looked at me and said, "You can tell that to the judge then." I said, "Fine," and stormed out of her office about as angry as I could be. Next thing I know I was in front of the judge and he asked me why I refused to go to rehab. I told him several reasons: one, I was in bankruptcy and I couldn't afford to pay $2,000 for rehab right then; two, I didn't have my driver's license and there was no one to bring me there;

three, I was self-employed and have a business to run. I actually thought I could persuade the judge to see things my way. Instead he said, "You got two choices: one, go to rehab for thirty days or two, go back to jail and finish the rest of your ninety days."

I told the judge, "Are you for real?" and walked out of there steaming mad. I went into rehab angry, mad, full of pride, and with a real attitude problem. The first two weeks of group discussions, my attitude was "You can make me be here but you can't make me participate." So when it came my turn to talk, all I said was my name and I chose to pass while everybody else had something to say. After two weeks, my counselor took me aside and asked me if I wanted to get my driver's license back. I said yes. He said, "I think you should know something then. I have to document how well each person participates in group discussions. And for whatever reason you choose not to is fine with me but it will not help you get your license back." After I heard that, the next day I started to participate and open up. I might have been mad and angry, but I wasn't going to be stupid on top of it. So I started to share the things that happened in my life that made me bitter and angry. After my counselor listened to me, I won't ever forget it because he was the first person who just listened without being judgmental. The next day he took me aside and said, "Rick, about those people you mentioned in your life that you're bitter and angry at—can I ask you a question about them?" I said yes. He said, "Do you think those people you're bitter and angry at are going around throughout their normal day thinking about you?" I said no. He said, "Then why are you going around thinking about them, causing you to be angry and bitter? When you do that, you're allowing them to rob you of being happy. You seem like you could be a real nice guy if you would just let go of all that anger built up in you." That was all it took for me to realize I was only hurting myself and no one else. Then he recommended that I forgive everyone and reconcile with the ones I can and get back to the relationship I once had with God. And that's what I did over twenty-five years ago. That day I let go of all my unforgiven bitterness and anger toward everyone who ever wronged me. I remember it was better than getting out of jail because I was freed from myself. I could not believe the effect that bitterness and anger can actually have on you. As soon as I let all that bitterness go, it was like a ton of bricks was removed off my shoulders and I just had a new heart transplant. That's the day I started to experience true peace and happiness in my life. Here's the funny thing about my rehab experience and how God works. Remember how my attitude was before I went in the first two weeks and when I told the judge I didn't have $2,000 to pay for rehab? The last two weeks I did a 180-degree turn around and became a model participant according to my counselor. On the last day I told him, "I think I need more time here but I can't afford it right now." He knew I owned a carpet cleaning business and he told me the rehab carpets need to be cleaned and asked if I would be interested in giving an estimate. I said yes, so he talked to the owner about me and my situation. The owner agreed and I ended up cleaning all the carpets in the rehab building which paid my $2,000 rehab bill. On top of it, they allowed me to come back for another two weeks free to make up for the first two weeks while I was being a jerk. Now I thank God for forcing me to go to rehab because that's what I needed, as you could see I would have never volunteered on my own. The scary thing is if I had my own way, I would still be that same bitter angry person today if God didn't step in with his rules and limits. What about you? Are you holding on to any unforgiving bitterness or anger towards anyone? If your answer is yes and you want to have peace and happiness in your life, Jesus says the first thing we need to do is forgive others. In Matthew 6:14,15, NIV, he says, "*For if you forgive other people when they sin against you, your heavenly father will also forgive you. **But if you don't forgive others their sins your father will not forgive your sins.***" Jesus also said, "If you have a dispute with your brother and you want to bring a gift to the altar, the first thing you need to do is leave your gift at the altar and go make it right with your brother and then come back and offer your gift to me." (Matthew 5:23, 24) In other words according to God, forgiveness is not to be taken lightly. In fact, it is the first major step to take before receiving anything from God. If you want God's peace, joy, and happiness, the first step towards that is getting rid of any bitterness you may have towards someone. And the only way to do that is by forgiveness.

Why waste any more time of your life like I did, letting someone else and the Devil rob you of the peace and happiness that God wants for you.

Are you blaming God or others for your problems?

I believe the biggest thing that keeps us from finding true happiness is our own selves. That's because we either blame God or others for most of our problems. And most of the time they're those who are closest to you like parents, spouse, family members, and friends. To be blunt, we are our own worst enemy most of the time, and our problems are caused by the poor choices we make. By nature, our first reaction is to blame someone else or lie to protect ourselves—let's be honest, we all do it. By blaming someone else, it allows us not to have to take responsibility for our own actions. And that is the Devil's game plan that he wants us to fall into. He knows as long as he can convince you to keep blaming someone else, you won't take responsibility for your actions. It's the oldest trick in the bible. In other words, the next time you decide to blame God or someone else for the problems you cause, you are allowing the Devil to keep you imprisoned by your own self like I did. And here's the crazy part: you're the jailer and you have the key to let yourself out if you want to. But as long as you keep playing the blame game, you will keep yourself imprisoned by whomever it is you're blaming. The key is face the truth and take full responsibility for your own actions. Always remember the truth is what sets you free spiritually. Why? Because the truth is the only thing that defeats the Devil. Remember after Eve ate the fruit, God didn't go to Eve first; he went to Adam because he was mostly responsible. Whenever I hear the story of Adam and Eve, it always seems like Eve gets all the blame for our sin problem just because she ate the fruit first. But if you study their story, the truth is God went looking for Adam first. Why? Because God gave the commandment to Adam before Eve was even created; in my opinion, Adam is more to be blamed. Eve may have eaten the fruit first, but I believe Adam was standing right next to her listening to the conversation she was having with the Devil. He could have stepped in at any time and said, "No, we're not eating anything from the tree God commanded us not to eat from. And he should have told the Devil to stop talking to his wife and hit the road. But instead I believe he liked what the Devil had to say so he kept quiet. Plus, he might have been thinking that if anything bad happened from God, he could always blame Eve because she ate it first. In other words, I believe she was like a guinea pig: he wanted to see what would happen without him eating it first. Then what did God do? He went looking for Adam first, not Eve, and asked him if he ate from the tree he commanded them not to eat. Adam not only blamed Eve but he also tried to blame God first. He didn't say "My wife deceived me," he told God "It was the woman that you gave me and she caused me to eat." In other words, he blamed both God and his wife. And after they sinned, God said to Adam, "Because you listened and did according to the voice of your wife, I'm going to curse the ground and you're going to have to work hard for your food now." In other words, God held Adam as the most accountable because he didn't step in; he played Dumbo Colombo and that doesn't work with God. Then God says to Eve, "What is it that you have done?" She doesn't take responsibility either: she blames the serpent (the Devil). This is where the blame game originated. Are you being deceived by the same serpent (the Devil) and blaming others for the problems in your life? I used to until I got tired of being deceived and paying for the consequences that go with it.

Are you in a snake pit situation?

I like to use the snake pit analogy because it reminds me of what my own situation once was. In other words, the snake pit can be a bad relationship, the wrong friends, alcohol, drugs, or anything that's not approved by God in your life. The snake bite is the bad consequence that goes along with playing with snakes. If you keep going around the same snake pit, you're eventually going to get bitten—it's just a matter of time. A lot of times we keep going back to the same snake pit and get bitten over and over again—that was me. And then we try to blame it on the snake; now, how foolish is that? The truth is if you hang around snakes or play with them, you're going to get bitten: it's the price we pay when playing with the Devil. If you don't like getting bitten, the solution is simple: stop going to the snake pit. It's not the snake's fault: you put yourself in that situation. It took me many years of unnecessary snake bites to learn that lesson. That's because I thought I could control snakes without getting bitten, but that never happened: I always got bitten somehow. The truth is all snake handlers eventually get bitten. They can be as careful as they want and still get bitten. In other words, we can't play with sin or control sin and expect not to get bitten by it. I thank God for stepping into my life with his grace and taking the snakes out of my life one by one. Because I was too powerless at the time to do it on my own, I would keep going back to the same snake pit as long as it was there. And I'm not advocating you wait around for God to do that unless you like getting bitten. The lesson here is simple: the sooner you stop going to the snake pit, the sooner you'll stop getting bitten by the consequences of sin. And going to a different snake pit isn't the solution either: I already tried that and the snakes bite there too. King Solomon says, "**A person's own folly leads to their ruin**, *yet their heart rages against the Lord.*" (Proverbs 19:3, NIV) That's one of the things that took me the longest time to learn. It was my own foolishness that was to blame for my problems, not others. That's one of the first steps to finding true happiness: stop blaming others for your problems, because you'll stay stuck there. In other words, you can't move forward to the next step until you become honest with yourself first. If you have any bad habits that are holding you back from true happiness, then ask God for help to get rid of them one by one or whatever it takes. And don't be deceived like I was and think you can even hold on to one snake (sin) and not get bitten. Here's the deal: God's outcome for sin is always the same, called bad consequences. And the only way we can change that is by making the right choices by listening to God and obeying His command-ments. In other words, our obedience to God opens up all His benefits He has to give, especially His peace, joy, happiness, and success, and that's real-ity. Insanity is when we sin against God and still expect a good outcome. The lesson to be learned is God will not allow us to have true happiness outside the limits of His approval. Solomon tried and couldn't do it. He thought happiness was in collecting and marrying foreign women. God warned him two times to stop because they would eventually turn his heart away from Him and worship other Gods. He ignored God's warnings and it made Him angry and paid a big consequence: he lost everything including his kingdom. Solomon learned the hard way: instead of using his wisdom, he kept going back to the same snake pit God told him to stay away from. Here's what I learned from Solomon and my own experiences of trying to find happiness outside of God's approval. I look at it like chasing the wind. You can't catch it, keep it, or hold it. In other words, you're just wasting your time when God makes it impossible to achieve. Once God revealed that truth to me, I stopped listening to the Devil's suggestions about happiness. I started listening to God, claiming His promises and studying everything He had to say about it. In short, what I learned and has helped me the most about finding true happiness is claiming God's promises. The bible says, "Happy are the people who put God first. And in my presence is the fullness of joy. My people will be happy and satisfied with my goodness." In other words, if you want to be truly happy, then God needs to be first and present in every aspect of your life. That's when He will show you His goodness and that's the key: His goodness is what makes us truly happy. You don't have to look for it or try to find it when He promises to give it to you. God will be the one to fill up your happiness tank with his goodness. He's not asking you to do it. On the other hand, the Devil who is evil doesn't have the capacity to give good things. The only thing the Devil can do is what God allows him to do. And that is to lie and deceive us by suggesting ways that can make us happy outside of God's goodness. And at the same time, God allows us the freedom to choose who you want to believe, God's promises or the Devil's lies. The bottom line here is you and your choice! That's one thing God or the Devil isn't going to do for you is make your choice. Here's the deal: when we practice sin against God, that sin is what keeps us from His Goodness. And God set it up so that the only thing that can truly make us happy is His goodness. And the Devil knows that truth more than the majority of the world, and his mission is to keep you from it. The Good news is Jesus wants us to be happy in every aspect of our life if we allow him in. Finally, ask yourself this question and it's the one I ask myself whenever I got tempted about something: When you know it's impossible for the Devil to give anything good with a successful happy outcome, then why waste your time being deceived by his lies? I learned that making the right choice is based on the reality of knowing what the truth is and the truth is what shuts down the Devil. In other words, when you start listening to Jesus, he's going to show you the truth and the way to a happy successful life. I can tell you one thing for sure: it's a whole lot better than the other alternative. Listening to the Devil's lies always leads us to a destructive unhappy end.

Key questions to ask yourself:

• Are you trying to find true happiness outside of God's approval limits?

• Are you letting any bitterness or anger rob you of God's peace and joy?

• Are you blaming God or others for your problems?

Key points to remember:

• True happiness and joy can only come from God and his presence.

• Trying to find happiness outside of God's approval is a waste of time.

• Any bitterness or anger will destroy your happiness.

God's promises to remember:

• Happy is that people whose God is the Lord. (Psalms 144:15, KJV)

• In your presence is the fullness of joy. (Psalms 16:11, KJV)

• My people shall be satisfied with my goodness. (Jeremiah 31:14, KJV)

CHAPTER 5

GOD KNOWS WHAT'S
BEST FOR YOU

I think one of the most ridiculous things we do as Christians is when we think we know what's best for ourselves than what God does. I believe that's the main reason why it's so easy for the Devil to deceive us. When we have the mentality that we know what's best for our lives, two things happen. One, we're placing ourselves as the god of our life instead of the God who created us. Two, we play right into the hands of the Devil. We're vulnerable to his tricks and lies when we don't let God show us what's best.

David reminds us of that. He says let us not forget *"that it is **He who has made us and not we ourselves.**"* (Psalms 100:3, NKJV) Why does David have to remind us of that? I don't believe anyone in their right mind really believes they created their own self, but we sure act and live like it sometimes. I believe David was saying keep things in their right perspective. The creation can never know more than its creator or what's best for it. He goes on to say we are the Lord's people and the sheep of his pasture. The Lord is our Shepherd and we are his sheep, and the sheep are supposed to listen and follow the shepherd's voice. The shepherd's job is to care for his sheep, making sure they are protected at all times and leading them to the best green pastures. That is the way Christians are supposed to live, following Jesus' voice and letting him lead us to the best things of this life. But I don't believe the majority of Christians actually do that. I know I didn't for many years. Remember he said there's only a few who follow him on his narrow road. That's because we want to find our own green pastures. And when we do that, we run into problems. Sometimes a sheep will wander off from its shepherd trying to find greener grass somewhere else and ends up getting into trouble. It can easily get caught in a thicket of bushes, fall in a pit, get lost, or killed by another animal. That's the risk we take when we want to go our own way to find what we think is best for us. The bible says there is a way that seems right unto a man, but the end results are the ways of death. In other words, what we think is right and best for ourselves is not the same as what God knows is best. When our ways are not aligned with God's ways, we fall short of experiencing his best in our life. Death means separation from God, so when we do things our way, we are actually separating our-selves from God and his best. When we decide to do things our way according to the bible, our best result is always going to be the same: a dead-end road to unhappiness. That's what happened to the prodigal son. He had a good life going for him, everything laid out for him by his father. Then one day he thought that wasn't good enough and had a better idea to live a more exciting life. He was of age so he asked his father for his early inheritance, took it, traveled to another country, and spent it all on the pleasures of this world. Life was great for a while until he ran out of money and there was a famine in the land. I don't think he was planning on that to happen. He was too busy living his life in the fast lane, the here and now. He's now broke with a famine in the land to top it off. Life for him in the fast lane just stopped. He's not enjoying the pleasures of this world anymore: he's just trying to survive. He finally ends up getting a job feeding and living with pigs and eating their food just to stay alive. One day he came to his senses and thought to himself, "My father's servants live better than the way I'm living in this pig pen. They don't have to sleep with the pigs and eat their food. They have plenty of good food to eat, even with extra to spare. If I stay here any longer, I'm going to die," so the next day he heads back to his father's house and tells him, "I really messed up with both you and God. I'm not worthy to even be called your son. I would be happy if you would be willing to take me back as one of your hired servants." He learned living life on the wide road to destruction isn't the best way to live after all. I can relate with his story when he came to his senses in the pig pen. Thank God I didn't end up like that, but that's how I felt when I was in bankruptcy and rehab at the same time. That's when my wild ways of living came to an immediate end because I ran out of money and I had no more credit. I said to myself, "How in the world did I end up here?" I can answer that now: I thought I knew what was best and did things my way. Living that way will eventually come to an end and it won't be a good one either. The best way to live is doing things God's way, always trusting that He knows what's best for you. The Devil likes to trick us to believe the grass is always greener or better somewhere else other than what God has already given us just like he did with Adam and Eve. I think we all have a little bit of the prodigal son in us when we think we know what's best for our life. I have learned that's a dangerous unhappy way to live while at the same time you're forfeiting God's best. On the other hand, when you listen and follow Jesus, you have the best resource in this world. He's always going to give what's best for you as long as you listen and follow him. Jesus doesn't promise he will always give you what you want but he will give you what's best. And the reason for that is his best is always going to be better than what you want in the first place. It's taken me a lot of years to learn that and still am. God's best is always better than what we think is best. For example, here's a funny lessen God showed me about thinking you know what's best. I like cats but I don't know why they don't listen and they don't do what you tell them. They do what they want when they want; maybe that's the attraction. My favorite is black cats. I've had three of them. One day my wife told me my daughter had another stray cat hanging around their house and wanted to know if I wanted it. I asked what color it was. She said, "Almost all white." I said, "No, thanks. You know I only like black cats and I already have one." My wife said, "Could you at least give it a chance?" I said, "No, there's no sense doing it. It's a waste of time when you know very well I only like black cats." She then reminded me that the black cat that my daughter gave me nineteen years ago has white paws. Then I reminded her even then I was reluctant to take her because of the white paws. I said, "There's no sense arguing about this cat. I know what I like." Then my wife made me a proposition. She said she was going to baby sit overnight at my daughter's. She asked if the cat could stay with me overnight as a test. And if I didn't like the cat, she promised she wouldn't bother me anymore about the cat. I agreed. It sounded like a good deal to me for two reasons. One, I knew I wasn't going to like the cat, and two, it would get my wife off my back. I told her, "Don't get your hopes up. God Himself would have to change my heart for that cat to stay." I was 99.9 percent sure that wasn't going to happen like I knew what God was going to do. So, then I was sitting on the sofa watching TV and the cat came in the room and looked at me. And I said, "I'm sorry. Don't get too comfortable cause you're not staying here." Then she jumped up on the sofa and laid on my lap and started purring. I was a little in shock because none of my other cats would ever sit on my lap. I didn't have the heart to shoo her off my lap, so I just let her sit there. I started to get tired and fell asleep on the sofa. When I woke up, the cat was sleeping on my chest. I couldn't believe it. I never had a cat or any animal show me that much love. At that point, it didn't matter to me what color the cat was. The cat got to stay and I swallowed my pride both to my wife and God. Now she always sleeps on my lap and chest. It's been the best pet I have ever had. God showed me a valuable lesson that day: don't think you know what's best. Keep an open mind and don't think you know what God's going to do even if your 99.9 percent sure. If you're a parent and you have children especially teenagers, then you must know how God feels about who really knows what's best. Of course that would be you when it comes to your children, but they don't always see it that way. They think your ways are old or out of touch and think they know what's best for them. The funny thing is as adults and parents, we think the same way about God. The reality is you have been on earth a lot longer than your children and have a lot more experience and wisdom to offer them like God does with us. As with any good parent, you want what's best for your children whether it's the school they go to, getting a job, buying their first car, or getting married. You know your child's likes and dislikes better than anyone in the world because you raised them. They might not always agree when they don't get your approval on something or get what they want. Then you become the bad parent as soon as you point out something that might not be good for them. Because they want it so bad, they are blinded by the possible consequences they don't see. They can't see the whole picture like you can because you've been down that road before. They don't realize that all you're doing is looking out for their best interest because you want them to be happy and have good success. God is no different: He wants the same thing for us; that's where we get it from. No matter how old you are, we are all children of God and he always knows what's best because he created you and knows everything about you. David said, *"You have searched me, you know when I sit and when I arise; you perceive my thoughts from afar. You discern my going out and my lying down; you are familiar with all my ways. Before a word is on my tongue you Lord know it completely. You hem me in behind and before, and you lay your hand upon me. Such knowledge is to wonderful for me. To lofty for me to attain.* (Psalms 139:1–6, NIV) We need to have that same mind-set as David had, reminding ourselves that God knows everything about us. And if you believe that, why not trust that God always knows what's best for you. He knows every detail of our life; even the hairs of your head are numbered. Do you know the exact number of hairs you have in your head? If not, I guess you don't know as much about yourself as you think. Jesus says a sparrow doesn't even fall to the ground without him knowing about it and how much more valuable and important are you than the sparrow? Think about it this way: would you want Jesus to give you what you wanted when you wanted it even if it wasn't best for you? And after he granted your request, he also let you peek behind the curtain to see what you missed out on. If God really allowed us to do that, we would be sad every single time because we missed out on something better. God is always going to win at that game. That's what I have found out like my cat lesson. In other words, God's best is always going to be better than your best, that's why I say it is ridiculous to think otherwise. I have learned this over the years. Instead of asking God for what you want, start asking him to give you what's best for you in every aspect of your life. Take God up on his promise. David said, "**Delight thyself also in the Lord, and he shall give thee the desires of thine heart.** *Commit your way to the Lord, trust also in him, and he shall bring it to pass.* (Psalms 37:4, 5, NKJV) He's the one who put those desires in your heart in the first place and He's the only one who can truly fulfill it. The key is you have to allow Him to show you what's best by trusting Him. And if you stay committed and wait on Him for his timing, he promises to fill up your happiness tank in every aspect of your life.

Jesus' best is always better

A good example of that is the first miracle Jesus did at the wedding in Cana when he turned the water into wine. They must have had a lot more people than what they planned for because they ran out of wine. That would not be a good situation to have happen at your wedding, especially if you were the bridegroom. The guests were starting to complain because there was no more wine to celebrate with. And before it started to get too widely known, Jesus' mother took Jesus aside and said, "The guests are starting to grumble and complain that there's no more wine." And Jesus said to her, "Why is this my problem?" I believe she responded by saying, "Just do it," because then his mother went over to the servants and told them, "Whatsoever Jesus tells you to do, don't ask any questions: just do what he says." I believe the reason she said that is she was ready to put Jesus to the test. In other words, she knew he would have to do some kind of miracle, because he surely didn't bring any extra wine to the wedding with him. Then Jesus told the servants to fill six water pots full with water. If I was there, I would have asked, "Why are we filling the pots up with water when we need wine right now? Somebody's got to go to the store fast." That would have been the most logical way to think about it.

The thing is if anybody did make a wine run, by the time they got back it would have been too late. Because Jesus already solved the problem by turning the water into wine, plus the wine wouldn't have been as good as his. Jesus said, "Okay, I did my part. Everything is all set. Let the master of ceremonies taste it first." And when the master of ceremonies tasted the wine, he didn't know where in the world it came from; only his mother and the servants really knew what happened. Then the master of ceremonies went over to bridegroom, who didn't have a clue of what's going on behind the scenes. And he said to the bridegroom, "Wow this wine is better than the first wine" and gives him the credit. Then he said, "On every wedding I've ever been to, the man always brings out the good wine first. And after everyone has drunk the good wine, they would bring out the cheap stuff; instead, you saved the best wine for last." The funny part to this story is no one in the wedding even knew what just happened and the bridegroom got the credit for Jesus' miracle. He had to be scratching his head thinking, "What in the world just happened? I don't remember buying or saving the best for last." But at that point it really didn't matter because everyone was happy, especially having the best wine for last thanks to Jesus and his best. The thing for all of us to learn from this story that I think gets quite often overlooked is Mary's role. If it wasn't for her compelling Jesus to solve the wine problem, the wedding wouldn't have turned out as well as it did. She was looking for a miracle, expecting a miracle, and she saw the miracle. Think about how many miracles we would see in our lives if we started thinking that way?

Are you looking for the perfect soul mate?

Most people want to share their happiness, ideally with the perfect soul mate for the rest of their lives. God wants the same thing for us. Unfortunately, it doesn't always end up that way. Why is that? I think there can be many reasons why relationships end. I' m not trying to be a relationship expert here either, I'm just sharing my opinion, my experience, and what worked for me. I believe the biggest reason is we choose our own mate without asking God to show us the perfect mate who's best for us. Then we go to the altar and ask God to bless the relationship. I thank God my first relationships didn't make it that far. You might be saying, "What's wrong about picking out my soul mate that I think is best for me?" There's nothing biblically wrong with it. The only thing I would say is that it's pretty risky. I say that because choosing a lifelong soulmate has to be the biggest decision one will ever make. What if that person you choose is not the one God had perfectly designed and planned for you like anything else in your life? And If that's the case, that means you would be missing out on God's best. That's why I say it's risky when we try to make God's plans fit our plans. The truth is that way never works out. That's like trying to take a square peg and get it to fit in a round hole. That's when we have it backwards. God doesn't work that way. He gets it right the first time. Abraham and Sarah found that out when they decided to make God's plans fit theirs. Their plan didn't work out and it still causes a lot of problems that still exist today. God always gives us the freedom to make choices and it always comes down to this: do you want to choose what you think is best or do you want to wait on God for his best? And that's always going to be the bottom line. I have learned that when you choose to ask God for his best, which means his perfect will and plan, you just eliminated the risk factor How? Whenever you forfeit your right to get God's best, then there is no risk involved. His perfect will and plan has zero risk because it will always come to pass and that's how you end up with His best. In the beginning relationships seem to always start out good just as long as you're both happy. In reality that doesn't happen every day and as soon as things aren't working out the way you expected, all of a sudden you're not sharing your happiness together anymore. That's usually when the relationship ends and you start over with someone else trying to accomplish the same thing. And when that doesn't work, you start over again. That's not God's perfect plan. I know all too much about that: growing up, my mother was married four times and my father five times. My goal here is not to be judgmental towards my parents or anyone else in similar situations. It is to help those who want to find a perfect soul mate to enjoy the rest of their lives with. Even if you're someone who has had one bad relationship after another, I believe with God it's never too late to start doing things the right way. For example, when Jesus talked to the Samaritan woman at the well, she was married five times. Jesus changed her life so much that she went and told everybody in the town about it. Then the whole town came out to meet him and many of their lives were saved and changed all because of one woman's testimony. In other words, it doesn't matter how many times you messed up: God can still use you to change other peoples' lives. Let me explain what I mean by God's perfect soul mate.

A perfect soul mate is not someone who is flawless; it is someone who God created perfectly, designed for you and only you. They are the only person in this world that God has patented with all the required qualities and characteristics to complete you. In other words, your mate is designed to bring out the best in you for the glory of God. No one in this world knows you better than God and your soul mate. On top of that, they are the only ones who can truly fulfill the desires of your heart. If you're someone who wants a perfect soul mate to spend the rest of your life with and still haven't found it yet, then the first question to ask yourselves is: are you trying to find that person on your own or are you asking God to bring that person into your life? That is the key to finding the perfect soul mate: being patient and waiting on God. I know waiting on God for something you really want can be difficult and unpopular, but I also know when you wait on His timing, you will always get the best. One thing is for sure: God knows exactly where your perfect mate is but you just don't know. He's behind the scenes putting the right people or situation in your life for you to meet. I have learned that when you wait on God and do things His way, one thing is for certain: you will always receive what's best for you. I know that from personal experience. That's how I met my wife and perfect soul mate for the first time.

By the time I was twenty years old, I was getting tired of the partying and bar life. The drinking age back then was eighteen. The relationships I had with girls never worked out. I was ready for a change in my life. I wanted to settle down and get married and not just to anyone. I wanted to do things right the first time and find the woman who was best for me, someone to spend the rest of my life with. My mother was recently divorced so I lived with her for a little while. Then I got kicked out for drinking whiskey in the house with my friend one day. I didn't have any place to live, so my best friend and his family took me in and let me live with them till I could get my own place. I thank God for them because my only other option was the street or living in my car. Even though they treated me like I was part of the family, it was the loneliest time of my life. All my friends were still partying and going to the bars which I really didn't want to do. It was either going along with my friends or sitting home by myself. I remember my heart felt like it had a big void; something was missing. For the first time I felt unloved because I had no girlfriend in my life. I knew all the girls in my school and the area I lived in and either I already dated them or none of them appealed to me. I didn't want to meet anyone in a bar so I told my friends to be on the lookout for a good woman who wasn't the partying type. I figured drinking and partying at the level I was doing was not a good way to start out a marriage. I had a few dates but nothing I was interested in. So here I was out of school, tired of partying and the bar scene. It seemed like all of the prospects for finding the right woman was exhausted because I knew them all—I lived in a small town. So for the first time in my life, I decided to put God to the test. I wanted to see if he was for real like Mary did with Jesus at the wedding. I had never read the bible so I didn't know about his promises then. The only thing I knew about God is that he sent his son Jesus to die for my sins so I could go to heaven to be with him. I accepted him as my personal savior when I was eighteen years old so I didn't know much about God at all other than a few bible stories I learned in Sunday school. So my first big prayer to God went something like this: "God, I believe about the miracles and things you did for people in the bible, but that doesn't do me no good right now. What I mean is I want to see you do something real in my life so I know you're a God who listens and answers." I figured God should know where all the girls are, especially the one that is right for me. That day I made a deal with God. I said, "I'm tired of living the way I've been. If you will prove yourself to me and bring the right woman into my life, one who already knows you as her personal savior"—I also added in that she's got to be good-looking too; in other words, fulfill the desire of my heart—"and if you do that, I will know you are a God who hears and answers and I will worship and serve you the rest of my life." In my mind back then, I figured I couldn't lose. If God brings me the right woman, I shouldn't have to worry about things not working out and getting divorced which I wanted to avoid at all cost. And if that didn't happen, I would just blame God like Adam did. As we already know, that doesn't work. My point is that's how I looked at it back then. Then about a month later, my best friend who I lived with at the time told me about this new girl who had just moved in I should check out. The town I lived in was small; everybody knew each other, so somebody new moving in was a big thing. I found out what her name was and that she was sixteen years old, just short of turning seventeen, and going to my old high school. So I went to the high school to see what she looked like and asked someone to point her out for me. When I saw her for the first time, she had the most beautiful sparkling blue eyes I have ever seen in my life. The only other eyes I've ever seen that looked close to hers was Elizabeth Taylor's. I wanted to meet her right then but she didn't have a clue who I was. I found out she had a younger sister who was friends with my best friend's brother that I was living with at the time. And I didn't even know it, so the next time she came over, I told her to ask her sister if she wanted to go on a blind date and she said yes. And on our second date, I asked her if she went to church and what her denomination was. It was the same as mine. Then I asked if she knew Jesus Christ as her personal Lord and Savior and she said yes. And then she told me how she had been praying for God to bring her the best soul mate. I couldn't believe what I was hearing. I knew then she had to be from God. We both did. Her parents liked me and I liked them. Everything seemed to be going just perfect except for one thing: she told me she wasn't ready to stop partying, but she wanted to keep on dating. She said to me, "You got to get it out of your system; I got to have time to get it out of mine." I said I understand how she felt, being only sixteen years old and four years younger than me. I told her if that's what she wanted to do that's fine, but there's no sense of us wasting each other's time and dating anymore. She said, "How come?" I said, "You know that's not what I want to do anymore. I don't see how this can work you partying and me not." I said, "It's your choice what you want to do." She said she still wasn't ready to give up partying. I was really bummed out. It wasn't what I was expecting her to say. I gave her a hug and kiss, left her house, and went back to my apartment. I remember it was one of the saddest days of my life, worse than the loneliness before I met her. Only God knows how bad I felt. I cried and complained to him. That night, my heart was broken again for the fourth time. I poured my heart out to God, asking him why he put me through this again. "I thought she was from you. Everything was going just perfect except for her not wanting to give up partying. I tried to do the right thing now I have to start all over again. I don't want to have to go through this anymore. God, why couldn't you just make this work out?" And right about then, the phone rang. It was her. Today, it remains the best phone call I ever got in my life. She told me she thought about what I said and didn't want to take the risk of losing me. And that she was willing to do her best and stop partying so we could be together and continue our relationship. I couldn't believe it. God answered my prayer right while I was praying and complaining. That day, I went from the saddest point in my life to the happiest guy in the world. The only time I was happier is when God gave her back to me through his miracle with her brain tumor. After I hung up the phone, I thanked God many times and I still do today. She is the main reason I worship and serve God. She is a constant reminder of the best gift God could ever give me. After that, we dated for six months and then got married. I was twenty-one, she was seventeen. We've been married now for forty-two years, through the good, the bad, and the ugly. God has blessed us with two wonderful children and five grandchildren. If there is any one thing I know for sure in this life, it is that we were a match made in heaven. The older I get, the more I realize how God fulfilled every desire of my heart with a woman perfectly made for me. God gave me more than I could have ever imagined or even dared to ask for, and I'll leave it at that. I will jokingly say this: be careful what you ask God, for he might just give it to you. Remember when I added to my prayer she's got to be good-looking? Well, God definitely gave me that and a whole lot more. I think God had a little fun with me when I said don't forget she has to have good looks. He didn't tell me about the trouble that comes along with it. I spent the prime of my life finding that out. In other words, being a watchdog over other dogs who wanted what I had. And when they got too close, it ended in a dog fight, if you get the picture. I can't complain though: if I had to do it over again and God said I'll give you your request but you will have to be guard dog, I'd still take the deal. Now that we're older, I can relax a little more. I don't have the stress of being on dog duty anymore. My most favorite verse is "**Delight yourself in the Lord, and he shall give you the desires of your heart.**" If I was a tattoo person like my wife, that's what I would have tattooed on my chest. I thought about it once, but I just don't like permanent things written on my body. I got nothing against tattoos, as my wife has plenty of them. I look at it as God tattooed that in my soul by giving me a beautiful wife and the best soul mate I could ask for. God kept His part on the deal; as you know, I didn't always keep mine about serving Him when I was living on the wrong road. I thank God for His abundant grace and mercy, because He had every right to take my wife during those years or at any time. Back then I didn't realize how serious God was about breaking a deal with Him till years later. Solomon said when you make a deal with God, you better pay it. For God has no pleasure in fools. It's better that you don't make a deal than to make a deal and not pay. I learned you don't make a deal with God, get the goods run off, and think He's going to forget about it. Hopefully, you're not in a lonely situation without family or someone to love you can share your life with. If you are someone in a situation like that, I know how that can feel; that's why I'm sharing my story with you. My encouragement to you is first of all know that God loves you and wants to be the one who fulfills those desires of your heart and He will if you ask him. Look at it this way: you can either approach God with an empty treasure chest and ask Him to fill it with what's best for your life, or you can fill it yourself with what you think is best. He gives us that choice. In my experience, the first choice is the best. God proved to me He's the best matchmaker in the universe. God knows the desires of your heart better than anyone because he put them there when he created you. The truth is I don't believe a person really knows the desire of their heart until God shows it to them anyway, like my cat story. You might be saying, "I have been praying and still end up in one bad relationship after another." I know the feeling: the same thing happened with me. That's because I thought I knew what was best for me. Then I asked God to please make those relationships work out. That's like filling your treasure chest up with things yourself and asking God to bless it all; that doesn't work. On the other hand, when He fills it, it's already blessed; all you got to do is thank Him and praise Him for it. Now as I look back, I see why He didn't grant my request when He had something way far better for me I just couldn't see at the time. I had it all backwards until I got tired of things not working out and said, "Okay, God, you find me the right one instead of me trying to find it." That's the difference. You might be asking how do you know for sure when God brings you the perfect mate? When God brings you the perfect soul mate, you both will know it. When you're praying asking God for his perfect will, he either closes doors or opens them. When you see all the doors open and there's a green light at every corner, that's a good sign. That's God's will telling you to go forward. One thing about a sign from God that I feel very strongly about is that your soul mate knows Jesus as their personal savior before you go to the altar. I believe the foundation of salvation is vitally important in any successful relationship if it's going to last the test of time. We already discussed earlier that the only things that last are the things that are built on the foundation of Jesus Christ. Marriage is tough enough more or less starting out on two different foundations or beliefs. That is the one reason why I and my wife are still married today. God gave me the perfect woman who was best for me because I know no other woman on planet Earth would have dealt with me and my problems. The bible says when we are joined to gather with the Lord, we become one spirit, the same way it should be with our soul mate: the two become one flesh. Before I go any further, I want to make sure I'm clear about one thing on this subject. Because I know there are some of you reading this who are in relationships with either a spouse or significant other who doesn't know the Lord as their personal savior. I'm in no way insinuating that you break off your relationship just because they don't know the Lord as their savior, because at this point you are the closest hope for their salvation. I have seen it work once in my own family. It just took about eighteen years for that person to make that decision. What I'm saying is until they made that decision, there was no spiritual unity. In other words, I believe the ideal situation in a relationship is to both start out with the same spiritual foundation. I'm sharing this more for those of you who aren't married yet or in a present relationship that are looking for a perfect soul mate like I was. I believe when the Lord makes a perfect match made in heaven, you will both know Him as your personal savior. It's not biblical; it's just my opinion based on my personal experience, otherwise why would you call it a perfect match? To me, a perfect match is something only God can make happen because He is the only one who is perfect. All my past relationships failed and never worked out because none of them were founded on the principles of God. That's why this last time I prayed and asked God to make sure this person knew Jesus first. I didn't want anything less than the perfect situation. I wanted God to have that part done. That way, I knew He was behind it, what I call an open door and green light. Because in my world growing up, I have never seen that work out when one person knows the Lord and the other doesn't. One goes to church, the other doesn't. It didn't seem like an ideal happy situation to me. I'm not saying that kind of situation can't somehow ever work out over time or down the road. I just didn't want to waste that time or take any kind of a risk. In other words, having one shot to do this right the first time. The bible says, "Be ye not unequally yoked together with unbelievers; for what fellowship has righteousness with unrighteousness?" (II Corinthians 6:14, KJV) To me, a match made in heaven is when God is behind it and not ourselves. If you're someone who is still looking and wants to have the perfect soul mate, I highly recommend God's perfect match services: all you have to do is ask, wait, be patient, keep your treasure chest open, ask him to fill it, and he will bring it to pass. One thing I've learned is that when God closes the door on something, don't get discouraged, upset, or complain; instead, be grateful. That means he's got something better for you. God's will and plan is always on time, and He knows what's best for you even though it might not seem like it at the time. The bible says, "***This is the confidence we have in approaching God; that if we ask anything according to his will, He hears us. And if we know that he hears us whatever we ask, we know that we have what we asked of him.***" (I John 5:14–15, NIV) In other words, God wants you to have confidence, be on the lookout, and know that He is going to bring the perfect soul mate into your life. He made me a believer and He promises to do the same for all those who call upon Him. The best part is you don't have to try to figure out how it's all going to work out. That's God's part. All you have to do is trust Him to give you what's best and watch and see how He works it out. In my opinion, there is nothing better in this life than to have a perfect soul mate. Specifically made for you from God to enjoy the rest of your life with and I hope the same happens for you.

Jesus always knows where the fish are

One of my favorite bible stories of God knows what's best is when Jesus asked Peter to go fishing. Try to put yourself in Peter's mind-set; especially if you're a fisherman, you should be able to relate to this story even more. Jesus was teaching the people on shore from Peter's ship while the other fishermen were cleaning their nets from a long hard night of fishing. When Jesus finished teaching, he tells Peter to go back out into the deep and go fishing again. Peter tried to tell Jesus there's no fish out there; he was fishing all night long working extremely hard with no success, not catching even one fish. On top of that, they just finished cleaning all their nets and equipment. What would you do if Jesus asked you to do the same thing? Would you have obeyed or called it a day? I hate to admit it but if it was me when I was younger, I would have called it day, knowing as much about Jesus as Peter did then. The Lord knows I don't have the patience to fish, period, much less go back out when you didn't catch a thing. And I would have missed out on this amazing miracle. I don't think Peter really wanted to go back out fishing either; he sure didn't sound like it. He told Jesus, "It's only because of your request I'm going back out there." Here was Jesus, a carpenter, telling Peter, a professional fisherman, how to fish. Can you imagine what Peter was thinking? How does a carpenter know anything about fishing? The funny part of this story is Jesus wasn't just a carpenter: he was the Son of God and creator of all things, including the fish. Peter didn't look at it that way. I think he looked at it like, "I do this for a living and I know what's best." I don't think Peter was looking forward to catching any fish at all as much as showing respect to Jesus and to prove he was right. Until Jesus told them to lay down their nets and they caught so many fish that their nets started to break. There was so many fish they had to call their partners who were fishing nearby on the other ship. And when they got there, they had to fill both ships to the point where they both started to sink. And when Peter saw what was happening, the first thing he did was fall down at Jesus' knees and said, "Depart from me for I am a sinful man, oh Lord." At first I said to myself, "Why did Peter react that way? He didn't do anything wrong. He obeyed Jesus when he told him to go back out fishing when he didn't want to." When he saw all those fish, I thought he would have been running around the ship praising Jesus and high-fiving everyone. Instead he falls down and admits he is a sinful man. I believe that's when Peter got saved because he calls Jesus "Lord" for the first time instead of "Master." When Peter saw all those fish, he wasn't only astonished: he realized for the first time he was fishing in the presence of Almighty God. Imagine yourself in Peter's shoes right then, catching the most fish you have ever seen in your life. To where the nets were breaking and the boats were starting to sink. Peter experienced three extreme situations that day. One was after he tried his best, they didn't even end up with one fish. The other was he was fishing with the Son of God, not just a carpenter. The other was he experienced a miracle of the most fish he had ever seen and caught in his life. Most importantly, Jesus proved to Peter that day and all them that was with him who they were really fishing with. They were so amazed at what Jesus did and the amount of fish they caught that when they got to land, they left their entire livelihood behind and followed Jesus. I'll tell you what: Jesus sure had to have blown their minds with that fishing experience. For them to just walk away and leave all their livelihood behind and not even take the time to at least sell it. My guess is they were in such a state of amazement they didn't want to let Jesus get out of their sight. They wanted to follow him to see what he was going to do next. That's what we need to do: if we want to experience the best of Jesus, we must follow him. When we decide to listen, obey, and follow Jesus like they did, we too will experience miracles and all kinds of amazing things along the way in our lives. I believe we can all have fishing experiences as Peter did in our own lives. In other words, we're all fishing for something to make us happy. For Peter, it was catching fish because that's all he knew. For me, it was fishing for the perfect soul mate. I don't know what you want or what you're trying to fish for. It may be the perfect soul mate, job, career, a home, place to live, or the best deal on something. Maybe you have been fishing for something a long time now and you're tired and discouraged because your net keeps coming up empty. I know how easily that can happen when we try to do things our own way. One thing I know for sure: Jesus knows what's best for you and where the fish are. The key is always invite Jesus into every aspect of your life and in all that you do. I have learned this over the years when you make that a practice every day. You will see more good and amazing things happen in your life like you've never experienced before. That's because it is impossible to walk close with Jesus and not see unbelievable miracles happen. The bible is full of them. Why not start making your life full of them? Remember, never underestimate what God can do in your life. Even when things look impossible, He can make all things possible. He says, "*Call to me, and I will answer you,* **and show you great and mighty things, which you do not know.**" (Jeremiah 33:3, NKJV) That is one powerful, bold promise. Why would anyone not want God to show them great and mighty things? I think the most logical answer to that is you would have to think you have something better in mind to pass that offer up. Remember Solomon started out letting God show him great and mighty things until he decided to show himself. That was a big mistake and we already know how that ended. Here's the key to that promise if you want to see God do great and mighty things in your life. He said "I will show you" and not the other way around. In other words, you have to put God first before yourself and wait on him to show you these things. And when we get impatient and go ahead of God, we miss out on his best every single time. Here's what I say about that: why don't you let God show you around this world and what's best for you? After all, he created this world, he created everything in it, he created you with a purpose plan and desires. That's why he's the only one who truly knows how to fulfill those desires and not ourselves. All God is saying is "Trust me and let me show you what's best and things that will blow your mind." He sure showed Peter and blew his mind that day, and he has blown my mind many times and I'm looking forward to a lot more. I wish I could stop here and share all those mind-blowing stories with you right now but I can't because that's a book in itself. I used to blow my mind with alcohol and drugs to achieve euphoria, now I let Jesus do that. I'll tell you there's no comparison. The difference I found is after reaching a euphoria of alcohol or any kind of drug, there's always a negative downside that goes along with it such as a hangover or withdrawal. On the other hand when you experience the euphoria of Jesus, there is no downside: it's called peace, joy, and happiness. You'll have to experience that out for yourself and I hope this book will show you how.

Key questions to ask yourself:

• How do you know what's best for you if you didn't create yourself?

• Are you willing to give up your ways for God's best?

• Will you trust God to fulfill the desires of your heart?

Key points to remember:

• It's ridiculous to think we know what's best for our lives over what God does.

• God knows everything about you; even the hairs of your head are numbered.

• God wants what's best for you in every aspect and detail of your life.

God's promises to remember

• Delight yourself also in the Lord and he shall give
You the desires of your heart. (Psalms 37:4, NKJV)

• This is the confidence we have in approaching God: that if we ask anything according to his will He hears us. And if we know that he hears us whatever we ask we know that we have what we asked of him. (I John 5:14–15 NIV)

• Call to me, and I will answer you, and show you great and mighty Things, which you do not know. (Jeremiah 33:3, NKJV)

CHAPTER 6

THE FIRST STEP: WHO'S FIRST, YOU OR GOD?

If we want to live a true happy and successful life full of joy, the first thing we need to do is look at our priorities and God's and see how they line up. Everyone has their own set of priorities, how they want to live their life each day whether it's good or bad. A priority is something that is regarded more important to you than another thing. In other words, a priority on a list is going to be more important than the next priority below it and so on. When we set up our priority list, the goal is to focus on what's most important first, accomplish it, and go on to the next. For example, I have three priority lists I go by each day: spiritual, business, and personnel. The spiritual one always supersedes the others because God's list is what's most important. I believe God has two priority lists that apply to all of us. The first one is our personal intimate relationship with him and how he wants us to walk with him each day. The second one is our external relationship: how we treat others. These last four chapters are going to be more about our relationship with God and His priority list for a successful happy life. The one thing I like about His priority list it's not long and complicated; it's short and simple. But at first it's not all that easy to do until you make it a habit of your life. Jesus tells us clearly what God's top priority is by commanding us to do two things in Mark12:30, 31. First thing is to love God with all your heart, with all your soul, with all your mind, and all our strength. And the second thing he says is like unto the first, you shall love your neighbor as like unto yourself. There is no greater commandment than these; in other words, the ultimate commandment. And if you can live by these two commandments, you got your priorities in the right order with God. Jesus said that is the ultimate commandment, which means that's God's number one top priority he wants us to do first before anything else. In other words, if we want his blessings in our life, we better obey his top priority: this is why I call it the first step. If we don't get God's first step right, then nothing else matters. For example, when God's own chosen people didn't keep his first commandment or as I call top priority, they suffered his judgments and consequences until they got tired of it and decided to turn back to His top priority which is Him. It doesn't matter whether you're one man or a nation: you can't bypass God's top priority and expect his blessings. For example, when your boss or supervisor has a top priority for you to do and you choose to do your priority over his, you'll either get chewed out about it or possibly fired. When I was young at my first job, I learned that really quick in my life. My boss had a top priority he always wanted me to do that I thought was totally stupid. So I didn't do it; then I would get chewed out every time and argued over it. I decided it wasn't worth it so I sucked my pride up and made sure his number one priority was fulfilled. We went from being enemies to friends. He ended up being the best boss I ever had. Our priorities don't supersede; the authority that is above us whether it's God or man. If you want a good relationship with your supervisor, the key is always satisfy their top priority the same it is with God. I bet you I read God's top priority over 100 times before I really understood it. I thought I did love God with all my heart, soul, and mind until one day God pointed out something I was missing. It was the word all I said "Wow, how in the world did I miss that?" Then that commandment took on a whole other meaning to me. In other words, it's easy to love God with part of our heart, part of our soul, and part of our mind.

But that's not what Jesus commanded us to do. He said we're to love God with all our heart, soul, mind, and body. In other words, the key here is the word "all," meaning we are to love God 100 percent with our whole being. When I first looked at it that way, I knew I wasn't even close to that. What about you? Take a moment and ask yourself that same question: do you love God 100 percent with all your heart, soul, mind, and body? If your answer is yes, that means you would have to be infatuated with God 24/7. The only one I ever read about that even came close to that was David. To me at that time that seemed like that is humanly impossible: how can anyone love God 100 percent 24/7? Then I had to ask myself why would God ask us to do something if it was impossible, especially his number one top priority? That's when I said to God, "If this is possible to do, then you're going to have to show me how—because I don't know anybody that can." That's when I started to make that my goal to work towards, because according to Jesus that is the ultimate priority and goal. The reason I say "goal" is I don't believe it's possible for anyone to accomplish that overnight. It's a daily process that takes time, and the only one that can show us how to do that is Jesus himself. He's the one who showed me how step by step day by day and year by year. Basically, this book is about God's number one priority: Himself and you broken down into four daily priority steps. I remember before I even started this first step, I asked God if we should love you 100 percent in every aspect of our life? It seems like we won't have any room to love anything else—why is that?

God is a jealous God

He said, "Go back and read what I said to Moses in Exodus 20:5; you missed something." It says, "Thou shall not serve or worship any other Gods for I the Lord your God am a jealous God." Once I read that, I said to myself, "Wow, I didn't know God was a jealous God. I never heard that before.' After all, when you're God, you can have anything you want and if you don't have it, just create it. In other words, back then I didn't fully understand how and why God is a jealous God. So I decided to study everything the bible had to say about God being jealous. I tell you what I learned a lot in fact God is so jealous he told Moses his name is jealous. (Exodus 34:14) And then he said I will be a jealous God for my holy name's sake. (Ezekiel 39:25) When God says his name is jealous, we better take it seriously and not overlook what makes him jealous. Here's what I learned: we are the only thing that makes him jealous. In other words when God is not first place in every aspect of our life, that means something else is. And whatever that something else is means we love that more than we love God when He is not first. For example, we can all relate to this if you have a spouse, girl friend or boyfriend whom you're in love with. Are they not supposed to be first place in your heart? Suppose you found out that they were cheating on you with someone else: how would that make you feel? The first emotion we get is jealous, which then turns into anger, rage, separation, divorce, and sometimes murder. In other words, when you are no longer first place in that other person's heart, you will not tolerate being second. If I can't have you, no one will; you're not sharing yourself with no one, period. That's exactly how God feels when He is not first place in every aspect of our life. Where do you think we get our jealousy emotions from? It wasn't until God had me look at it from that perspective that I understood His; then it was clear as a bell and I hope it is for you too. In other words, when I understood the jealousy of God in my own life, it answered my question why we need to love God with all our heart, soul, mind, and body. In other words, God loves us with a jealous love, so much that he sent his son to die for your love. Once I finished my study and realized the gravity and scope of God's jealousy, I started to put God first place in every aspect of my life. In other words, the last thing I needed was a jealous God looking over top of my life. It's the best decision one can ever make, because how can you go wrong fulfilling God's number one priority? You can't. God also revealed to me another important reason why He needs to be first in all aspects of our life. Because if He's not first, then you will be first filling your heart, soul, mind, and body up with the things you love. And the things we love replaces God's love; that's when we start to become self-sufficient within ourselves and start following our own will and plans instead of His. We can't fully love God unless He is first place in every aspect of our lives. God is the only one that is truly self-sufficient; He doesn't need anything—we need Him. For example: when we love Him with all our heart, then His love abides in our heart, which allows us to love others. Without God's love in our heart, we don't have the capacity to do that on our own. The bible says our sin nature doesn't allow us to do good on our own. The apostle Paul said, "When I find myself to do good, evil is always present"; that's why we need to be filled with God's love and spirit. When we love God with all our soul, He's the only one who knows how to satisfy it. (Isaiah 58:11) What's our soul? I believe it's the spiritually aspect of our life; in other words, our personality, emotions, will, and what makes us happy. When we love God with all our mind, He will direct our thoughts. (Proverbs 16:3) When we love God with all our strength, He will allow us to do things we could never do in our own strength. (Philippians 4:13) In other words, unless we love God in all those areas first, we will be insufficient and lacking what we need to live a truly happy and successful life. The first step is asking yourself who's priority list are you living by each day, yours or God's? In other words, who's really first? That's always going to be the bottom line and top line with God that's never going to change. In Matthew 6:31–34, Jesus makes it perfectly clear what we are supposed to do first every day and what our top priority should be.

Seek first God's Kingdom

He starts out by telling us about the things we worry most about each day, like what we're going to eat, drink, and the cloths we're going to wear. He says the rest of the world worries about these things. But when you're a child of God, you don't have to worry about that. Your heavenly father already knows that you need all those things as well. Then Jesus tells us what we really need to be concerned about: "*Seek ye first the kingdom of God, and his righteousness and all these things shall be added unto you.* (Matthew 6:33, KJV) On the other hand when we focus on ourselves first before God, we have our priorities backwards. Why? Because He is all sufficient and we are insufficient. He is the true supplier of all our needs, not us. God knows we can't help but think about ourselves first, because it's our human nature. Our first priority step is to seek God first before anything we do, plus it keeps the Devil at bay. One thing not to overlook here is the word "seek," which means "search out" and "look for." In other words, we should be finding out as much as we can about God and his kingdom. This is where God's daily priority list starts. Whose kingdom is first, yours or God's? This is right where I started over twenty-five years ago after I messed my kingdom up. Since then, God has shown me how to make his priorities my priorities in four daily steps for living a happy and successful life. It has changed my life, my family's life, and I believe it can change your life when you make his priorities your priority. King David is a perfect example of someone who made God his number one top priority in every aspect of his daily life. He loved God with all his heart, soul, mind, and strength. He was totally sold out to God and infatuated with him 24/7. That's why he was the most successful king in the bible, because he sought after God like no one else did. That's why I decided to study his life more than anyone else's. I wanted to find out what he did to be so successful and why God called him a man after his own heart and no one else in the bible. I also wanted to know how he was so confident and bold, especially his success with killing Goliath at such a young age. As I mentioned earlier, I did not have a godly father to look to for answers or any godly mentor or role model. So I chose David because I wanted to know how to have that same kind of success he did. If someone is truly successful by God's standards, then all you have to do is copycat the same Godly principles as they did. For example, if you were taking a test and you were going to cheat, would you copy the answers from the A student or would you copy the answers from the D student? If you wanted to pass the test and have success, you'd copy from the A student. I hope you get my point without advocating anyone to cheat on a test. In other words, King David is what I call God's A student because he practiced God's first commandment better than anybody. The key to

David's success wasn't money, power, fame or certainly not his stature for he was just a little man. It was the fact that he had the power of God in his life and upon his life and I believe anyone can have the same thing. You just have to do the same thing he did which is not an easy thing to do especially nowadays with all the distractions we allow into our lives. The bible says David sought after the Lord's strength and his face continually. David did then just what Jesus is telling us to do today, to seek God first before anything. Not just going to church one hour on Sunday or whenever you feel like it, but consistently every day. David said, *"There is one thing I have desired of the Lord, that I will seek after; that I may dwell in the house of the Lord, all the days of my life."* (Psalms 27:4, KJV) The truth is David shouldn't be any more special than we are, yet God said he was because of his heart's desire to seek after him the way he did. I don't know if there's ever been a man who sought after God more than David did. But I do believe a man at the very least could copy him if his heart wanted to. And that is a key question: do you want to? If yes, David started his day by putting God first every morning before anything he did. He said, *"**In the morning I will direct my prayer unto thee and will look up.**"* (Psalms 5:3, KJV) and in verse 12 he says, "Surely, Lord you bless the righteous; **you surround** *them* **with your favor as with a shield.**" (Psalms 5:12, NIV) David didn't make a move without acknowledging God and putting him first. That's because he wanted to make sure he had God's approval, favor, and protection before he went forward on anything. Except for his sin with Bathsheba and murdering her husband, of which he paid a great sin consequence with his family. The lesson for all us to learn from this is not even the man after God's own heart gets a free pass for his sin. Don't copy that part; it didn't work for him and it's not going to work for us. That's why I only focus on the positive things he did that does work.

Set God first before anything you do

David said, *"**I have set the Lord always before me**: because he is at my right hand I shall not be moved."* (Psalms 16:8, KJV) Notice the key here is he always set the Lord before himself first. In other words, it was God who gave him all of his success. David never lost one fight or battle he was ever in, including killing a bear and lion with his own hands. And his most famous victory over Goliath the giant warrior we all know about. And he did all that while he was yet a young boy, all without a scratch on him. When I first learned that about David, I said, "How in the world can that happen?" Until the day I read Psalms 16:8, David answers that question and I believe it's the key to all of his success and our success. David is telling us, "If you want to know why I'm so successful, then here's what I do: I always set the Lord before me first before anything that I do. And I can always count on God being right there by my side. God is the one who gives me the victory over all my enemies and opposition. That's why I can boldly say I shall not be moved." The amazing thing about David is he learned that key principle at such a young age. That when you set God in front of you, no matter how big or bad your opposition is, it has to go through God first to get to you. My favorite example for that is when David killed Goliath, he never mentions or gives credit to his slingshot. Instead, he tells Goliath, "You might be big and bad, but you're no match for my God. You come to me a little shepherd boy with a sword a spear and a shield. But I come to you in the name of the Lord and he is going to deliver you into my hands. And then I'm going to kill you, cut your head off, and feed it to the birds so the whole earth will know who the real true God is." In other words, God was the real weapon that David announced would defeat Goliath, not his slingshot. We can have that same kind of confidence and success in our lives as long as we practice the same principle as he did. When you set God first before you each day like David did, you got priority number one in the right order. That is the key that opens up God's vault to his favor and success. It will show up in everything that you do like finding the right job, place to live, home, right soul mate, etc. Another crucial thing David did and talked a lot about his success is he learned to wait patiently on the lord. In Psalms 27:14, KJV, he says, "**Wait on the Lord and be of good courage and he shall strengthen your heart wait I say on the Lord.**" When he says "wait" twice in one verse, it means it's important and he doesn't want us to forget it. In other words, when you set God first, you also have to wait on his timing for things in your life. That for me has always been the hard part and I think it is for most people, waiting on him for his timing. I've been copying this same principle David did for years, set God first and wait on him to open the door. I have found it's the safest, most successful way to live when God opens the door instead of yourself. I don't go forward with anything in my life unless I know God is behind it first. That drives my wife batty a lot of times, but she knows it always works out in the end. When you open the door, it can be a risky scary thing when you don't know for sure what's behind it. When it just might be the Devil in disguise, and I've opened up enough doors to know that. The bible says, "Don't be surprised; Satan himself can transform into an angel of light." That's the scary part. On the other hand, when you wait for God to open the door, it's not risky or scary when you know Jesus is behind it. I have learned he is never too early and never too late; he's always on time with what you need and when you need it.

How do you start your day?

A lot of Christians get up each morning, get dressed and eat breakfast, and rush off to work without spending even one minute with God first. Recent studies say that approximately 90 percent of Christians don't read their bible on a regular basis. And the number one reason is they're either too busy or they don't have enough TIME! That used to be my excuse years ago; actually that is the oldest excuse in the world. The fact is that excuse won't work on God because he gives us all the same equal amount of time each day 24 hours. He also gives us the choice on how we want to spend that time. And time is how we show our love to God by what our priorities are and what we spend it on. The first thing we need to do is realize how important our time is to God. In fact, it is so important that we all have a personal appointment with him one day about how we use it. That appointment is called the judgment seat of Christ as we already discussed earlier. And I believe the number one topic is going to be about how we spent our time on earth. Even more than about our money. Why? Because time is the one thing we all have whether we have money or not. How we spend our time is more important to him than anything we do. That's why God created you so he could spend time with you to know him and his will for your life. The question is how much time are you spending with him each day? Time is a sacrifice and a gift. The most important thing a person can give someone is their time. Because once it's given, it can never be replaced like money and things. We've all heard the old saying "Time is money"; the truth is time is more valuable than money or any commodity in the world. How you spend your time speaks louder than words and shows how important someone or something is to you. No matter what age you are, we should all take a serious look at how we spend our time. Because once that opportunity of time is gone, it can never return the same way again like the water in a stream. You can lose your money and possessions and those could be replaced, but time is the one thing in life that never can be. That's why we need to use our time wisely each day because our days are numbered. If we want to please God, then we have to give him our time. The bible says, "*I beseech you therefor brethren, by the mercies of God, **that ye present your bodies a living sacrifice holy, acceptable to God, which is our reasonable service.**"* (Romans 12:1, NKJV) In other words, the sacrifice of our bodies and service to God is our time. This is a reasonable thing to do in comparison to what Jesus went through dying on the cross for our sins. In other words, imagine if you were standing next to Jesus before he went to the cross and he gave you a choice and said, "I will take your place and die an agonizing death on that cross for your sins if you in turn will sacrifice your time and body for my service to glorify God with." What would your choice be if given that alternative right at that moment? The truth and reality of that choice faces every one of us every day. The problem is we don't take time to look at it that way, but that still doesn't change what we're supposed to do in return. The bible says we were bought with the price of his blood for one reason. That is to glorify God in your body here on earth, which requires your time. We are God's servants, that's why we need to remind ourselves of that every day by putting him first in everything that we do. A servant doesn't put himself first over his master; he spends his time doing the things that are going to please his master. That's how we need to start our day, with that kind of mindset. The truth is we spend our time like we do our money—on what we want or what's important to us. Let's be honest: we all do it. In other words, to tell God you don't have time for Him is like saying, "You're not as important as other things." Yet we still want Him to bless us, our family, and everything else in our life. Sometimes we treat God like He's our genie: just rub the lamp when we need him. One thing is certain: everyone will make sure they have enough time to put their cloths on before they go to work. Make sure your makeup is on, your hair is combed just right, and your belly is full. We make sure we are physically prepared for the day but we neglect the most important part: being spiritually prepared. God gave you a spirit you have to take care of just as well as your body. And the only way you can take care of that is by reading his word.

Are you reading God's word every day?

Jesus said, "***Man shall not live by bread alone, but by every word that proceedeth out of the mouth of God.***" (Matthew 4:4, KJV) In other words, Jesus is not saying that as a suggestion, recommendation, or an option: it's a commandment. If you're a Christian and you don't take time to read God's word, Jesus is saying you are spiritually dead. The truth is the only reason you're physically living is you're eating and drinking or else you would be dead. The same is true spiritually if you don't read God's word every day. In other words, Jesus is saying we cannot live a true healthy successful life without feeding both our spirit and body. The truth is we don't think about taking care of the most important part first, our spirit. I think that's partly because we don't see it as important like our body. Why? Because we can skip reading God's word and still live physically speaking as opposed to not eating. If you're not reading God's word every day, then you're not really living because you are neglecting the most important part of your being, your spirit. Your spirit is part of God's kingdom which is his top priority. That's why Jesus said, "Seek first God's kingdom over anything else we do." Jesus talked more about God's kingdom than any other subject because that's what our life should be all about: his, not ours. If you haven't been reading God's word on a daily basis or maybe not at all, then this is the first place to start if you want to live a happy, successful life, having God's priorities in the right order. For example, physically speaking most people eat three times a day—breakfast, lunch, and dinner. Experts say the most important one is eating a good healthy breakfast before you start each day. That's because it gives you the right fuel and energy you need and the time to burn off the calories. Likewise, prayer and reading God's word gives you the spiritual energy and awareness of his presence. Most importantly, the number one way God speaks to us is through his word. I'm going to give you a few verses that really impacted me years ago, which got me started reading his word. But before I do, we first need to realize how powerfully important it is. Jesus said "I am the bread of life and the flesh profits nothing. The words I speak to you are spirit and life." In other words, everything lives, breathes and exists because of God's word. The only reason we exist and are breathing right now is because of his word. Stop and take a few minutes and look around you: everything that you see, hear, touch, taste, and smell all happens because God said so by his word. The bible says, "*In the beginning was the Word and the Word was with God, and the Word was God. He was with God in the beginning. Through him all things were made; without him nothing was made that has been made.* (John 1:1–3, NIV) In other words, if all things are made by his word, then all things can only live by his word and most importantly you over anything else. It also says that "*heaven and earth shall pass away, but my words shall not pass away.*" (Matthew 24:35, KJV)

In other words, Jesus is saying, "Everything I have created will eventually pass away one day except for my words; they will never pass away." The bottom line is God created us by his word, he commands us to live by his word, and we shall be judged by his word. (John 12:48) In other words, the only way we can truly live a successful happy life is by God's word. Just like eating the right food, it's not a option if you want to live a healthy life. Here are those verses showing what God has to say about reading and knowing his word.

My people are foolish, they have not known me, they are silly children; and they have no understanding. They are wise to do evil; but to good they have no knowledge.

(Jeremiah 4:22, NKJV)

*My people are destroyed **for the lack of knowledge.***

(Hosea 4:6, KJV)

*Also, **it is not good for a soul to be without knowledge.***

(Proverbs 19:2, NKJV)

Are you not in err because you know not the scriptures or the power of God?

(Mark 12:24, NIV)

Study to show thyself approved unto God.

(II Timothy 2:15, KJV)

***Till I come give attention to reading,** to exhortation, to doctrine.*

(I Timothy 4:13, NKJV)

Blessed is he who reads** and those who hear the words of this prophecy, **and keep those Things which are written in it, for the time is near.

(Revelation 1:3, NKJV)

Why do we need God's word every day?

There are four main reasons why we need to read God's word every day. The first is it's a commandment as we already discussed. The second is it's the only way we can grow spiritually and to know all about God and his ways. The third is it is the only way we can know what God's promises and benefits are so we can claim them upon our life. The fourth is it's the only way we can stay connected to Jesus, to follow his plans, directions, and joy in our life. I'm sure there are many other reasons but those I found to be the main ones. One of my favorite verses, the one that changed my life and the reason it's the title of the book, wherein Jesus covers it all in three categories where he said, "*I am the way, the truth, and the life.*" (John 14:6, KJV) In other words, if you don't have any direction in your life, Jesus is the way. We'll talk more about that later. If you're unsure or don't know what the real truth is, you don't have to rely on anyone else because he is the truth. And if you're someone who feels like life is not going very well for you right now, then I got some good news for you: Jesus is the abundant, joyful life. And I've got some even better news: Jesus tells us exactly how to live that life. I don't know of any other scripture in the bible where he explains it as well as in John 15:4–14, KJV. Jesus says, "**Abide in me and I in you**. *As the branch cannot bear fruit of itself except it abide in the vine, no more can ye except ye abide in me. I am the vine and ye are the branches:* he that abideth in me, and I in him, the same bringeth forth much fruit, **for without me you can do nothing.** (v.7) *If ye abide in me, and my words abide in you,* **Ye shall ask what ye will and it shall be done unto you.** (v.8) *Herein is my father glorified, that ye bear much fruit; so shall ye be my disciples.* (v.11) **These things have I spoken unto you, that my joy might remain in you, and that your joy might be full.**" (v.14) This covers everything in a nutshell why we need Jesus and his word every day. Because he is all in one; he has everything you need to live a truly successful life full of joy. In my opinion this is one of the most vitally important scriptures in the bible. Because Jesus gives us complete instructions what we need to do to live a joyful life. Because of that I am going to unpack it and break it down so it's a little easier to understand. Jesus says "I am the vine and you are the branch and without me you can do nothing." We all know what happens when a branch on a fruit tree breaks and separates from the main vine. It can't live very long by itself because it's not able to get the water and nutrients it needs from the main vine to bear its fruit. The branch eventually dries up and dies, and becomes good for nothing but kindling wood. The main thing Jesus is telling us here is we need to stay connected to him if we want to live a fruitful life, which is a successful life. He also tells us apart from him, we can do nothing which is not successful. That is the part that really got to me when I read it years ago. Without him, you can do nothing. What does Jesus mean by that? In fact, we can do a lot of things we want without him. What I believe he is saying here is about two things: one, we can't bear fruit to glorify his Father with, and two, we can't be filled with his joy without him. In other words, it's impossible to live a life full of joy and glorify God if you are not continually connected to Jesus. This is what made a big change in my life when I realized this truth. You can't bypass Jesus and expect to live a successful life full of joy. And here's the truth of the matter: at best we can be successful and make ourselves happy now and then. But that doesn't last all the time. It eventually ends and we're left wanting more. The one thing we can't do is fill ourselves with the joy that can only come from Jesus. Are you wondering like I did what's the difference between being happy and being filled with joy, and are they the same? This is what I believe the difference is: we can be happy about all kinds of things for a little while, but it doesn't last. Then we start looking for something else to make us happy again. And it's usually something that always goes our way or we wouldn't' be happy. Since things don't go our way all the time, then we can't be happy all the time. The reality is we can't be experiencing happiness all the time. On the other hand, the joy that Jesus is talking about is something entirely different, one that you can be full of all the time. Notice he says it's his joy that might remain in you, that your joy might be full. Jesus wants his joy to not only remain in you; he wants you to be filled with it every day. And that's the difference:

Jesus doesn't promise us happiness every day but he does promise we can be filled with his joy. In other words, no matter what our day brings, we can have Jesus' joy in us because it's not based on our circumstances. The key is we have to stay connected to him continually every day. If we break away and don't stay connected to Jesus, the joy in our life will eventually dry up and wither away. God's main purpose is for us is to bear fruit, not to be used for kindling wood. So the question is how do we stay connected to Jesus? In verse 7 he tells us how, with a promise and benefit with it. If you dwell in him, then his words dwell in you. You shall ask what you will and it shall be done unto you. The key here is Jesus' words that need to dwell in you; that's how you stay connected. And the only way you can have Jesus's words dwell in you is you have to read about him. "This is how my father is glorified, that you will bear much fruit." Notice Jesus didn't say "some fruit," he said "much fruit" or a lot of fruit. In other words, God has big plans for you to be successful for his glory. Jesus is saying our main purpose in life is to bear fruit and glorify God, not ourselves. The bible says no flesh will glorify themselves in the presence of God if anyone wants to, let him glory in the Lord. The fruit Jesus is talking about here I believe can mean a number of things. I believe anything that you do that is good and approved by God glorifies Him. Most importantly, fulfilling His purpose and will for your life and helping others. Finally, Jesus says in verse 14, "If you want to be my friend then do what I just commanded you to do."

How close are you to God?

How close of a relationship do you really have with God? The answer to that question is always going to be between you and him. What I'm getting at is this: a lot of Christians may say God is number one in their life. Saying it is one thing; living it is another. In other words, if God is really number one, then he needs to be first in everything that you do in order to have a close relationship with him. Years ago I would have told you God was number one in my life, only because I wasn't an atheist or didn't worshiped any other god. The truth was he wasn't always first and I didn't have a close relationship with Him like I thought. I prayed at meals and went to church, but that was about it. Back then God seemed like a galaxy away compared to now. It wasn't until I started reading and studying His word that my life started to really change. The most important thing I have learned about being close to God is He's only going to be as close to you as you are to Him; that's the bottom line. God does not force Himself on people; you have to come to Him. The bible says in James 4:8 if you come close to God He will come close to you. Notice that you have to make the first move. In other words, if you give God 5 minutes, He'll be close to you for 5 minutes. You give God 1 hour, He'll be close to you for 1 hour. You want to be close with God all day, He will certainly be close with you all day and that's the ultimate goal, 24/7. Our number one priority and focus should be God's number one priority, His first commandment. In other words, He wants to be first and present in every aspect of our life which is not hard to do when it becomes your top priority. And He will show us how to do that in these last four chapters. And here is the funny thing about the excuse of not having enough time to spend with God. You don't have to read your bible and go to church to find Him. If you know Jesus as your savior, his holy spirit is already in you no matter where you go or what you do he's there. The key in finding God is you don't have to look for Him; you just have to be aware of him. God is everywhere and in everything, and most importantly in you. Reading the bible and going to church is all good but that's no favor to God because it's a commandment. In fact, I don't believe we can do any favors to Him other than obey His commandments, most importantly the first one. Years ago I probably gave God about 5 minutes of my time a day if even that. My excuse was the same as everyone else's: I was too busy. The real reason is I was lacking in the understanding and knowledge of the word of God all because of my 5-minute relationship. And because of that, I didn't have a clue to all His benefits and promises I was missing out on. That's one thing I want to point out about obeying His commandments: there's always benefits behind it. In other words, God doesn't ask or command us to do any-thing without any reward or direct benefit behind it, and that's what motivated me to read. That's when I started claiming God's promises which led to having a 24/7 relationship. I learned the closer I got to God, the closer He got to me with His favor, goodness, and blessings. Once you experience that level of intimacy with God, you won't want to go backwards. Because you won't want to miss out on one moment of God's favor in your life. In other words, it's impossible to walk with Jesus all day and not see his favor or goodness show up in your life somewhere. Jesus spent his whole time on earth looking for opportuni-ties to help someone in need in some miraculous way. Think about the opportunity and privilege we have to walk with him today. As opposed to back then, people were climbing up trees cutting holes in roofs and plowing their way through mobs of people just to get a glimpse or touch him. We have it easy; we don't have to do those things. All we have to do is be aware of his presence through the Holy Spirit in us, which we'll discuss more about later. One thing Jesus is never going to say to you is he doesn't have enough time because of his busy schedule today. The first step in getting our priorities in the right order with God is by seek-ing him first thing in the morning like David did. God says, "*I love them that love me, and those that seek me early shall find me.*" (Proverbs 8:17, KJV) I believe everybody has at least 10–15 minutes to read God's word or an inspirational book before you start your day. It's all about making the time and not excuses, and sticking to it till it becomes a habit. Remember God's keeping the record books about how we spend our time. And He knows everybody has the time to do what they want. If you want God's favor in your life, seek Him before you start each day. Jesus said we need to prove our love to him by seeking him first. I can assure you by my personal experience and God's promises if you follow the four steps in this book God has shown me, your life will start to change, especially when you see God's favor and success show up in every aspect of your life. One thing to remember is after you pray and read God's word before you go to work or start your busy day, don't leave God at home in your devotional time box; take him with you and start talking with him throughout your day. Prayer and reading God's word is just to jump-start you. It spiritually wakes you up and prepares you for your daily walk with Jesus. And if you're a super busy person who works hard and long hours like I used to, then it's even more you need him. I'll bet your day will go a lot easier with Jesus than without him. Listen to what Jesus promises to those who work like that every day. Jesus said, "**Come unto me all you who are weary and burdened, and I will give you rest. Take my yoke upon you and learn of me, for I am gentle and humble in heart, and you will find rest for your souls.**" (Matthew 11:28, 29, NIV) Jesus is talking to everyone in the work field who works hard with busy schedules and heavy workloads. And if that's you, listen to what he promises. He says if you take his yoke upon you and learn about him, you will find true rest unto your soul. I'm going to unpack this promise because it's another one that made a major impact that changed my life. But before I do, I need to tell you this story first because most of my life I was an extreme workaholic and working fool in my younger years. Back then, I didn't know what the true meaning of rest even meant. Back when I was young, I thought taking time off from work was for lazy people. That's how foolish and extreme I was. I used to take the vacation pay from my job as a bonus and still work that week. Everything I did was all about work, work, work; every day for me was going 100 miles an hour. Until one day when I was twenty-five years old and I had a mental breakdown. That stopped me in my tracks. I thought I had mono because I was weak and had to sleep 12–14 hours. I could hardly make it to the mailbox and back without getting tired, so I went to the doctor. He examined me and said I was perfectly healthy except for me sleeping 12 hours and resting all day. So he started asking me questions about my job, the hours I worked and what I did all day. After he heard that, he said, "Who do you think you are, Superman? You can't do all that." He said my problem was my brain was so stressed out that my body is trying to catch up with it and it can't, that's why I was so tired. I said, "Okay, what kind of pills do I have to take and when can I get back to work?" He said, "There are no pills other than rest." I said, "How long is that going to take?" He said, "It could be six to ten weeks, whenever your body decides it's ready to catch up with your brain." I couldn't believe what he was telling me. I thought he was out of his mind. I said, "I can't afford to take that much time off from work. There has to be something I can take to hurry this up." That's when he took a wash towel, twisted it, and showed me, saying, "This is what your brain is like right now." Then he released the towel and as it started to slowly unwind, he said, "Only physical and mental rest can do that. And there is no speeding that process up." Before I left, he asked me if I had a priority list. I said, "No, what's that?" "It's a pad of paper where you right down your top priorities of things you need to get done for each day." He said that's part of my problem: I got way too many things going on around in my head. And if I wanted to recover sooner, I needed to take those things out of my head and put it on paper. I couldn't wait to get home and tell my wife what the doctor said, that I thought he was a quack and out of his mind. Actually, I was the one who was out of my mind. A long story short, I did what the doctor said because I really had no choice. And it took about the same time the doctor said it would for me to recover and return to work. That's when I realized he did know what he was talking about. That was when I first started my priority list and have been doing it ever since. How I went from that extreme to where I'm at today is hard for me to even comprehend. The only answer is reading and studying God's word over and over again, especially Matthew 11:28–30. Otherwise I would never have been able to enjoy the rest Jesus promises. The yoke Jesus is talking about here is a wooden crosspiece used to keep two animals together. The purpose was so the two oxen could pull evenly together heavier loads a lot easier than one by himself. In other words, how do we apply that to us today? I believe that wooden crosspiece (the yoke) is Jesus putting his arm around our shoulder. And him saying, "Take me to work with you and learn about me and my ways. I will make your job go a lot easier than without me because I am easy. That's when you will find my rest unto your soul."

And here's the big thing Jesus taught me about allowing his yoke and arm to be around you. You can't run or be in a hurry; all you can do is walk together. The key about Jesus' rest and easy workload is he never runs or hurries to do anything; he always walks. And guess what? He's always on time for everything and so will you when you're yoked together. When you're yoked to Jesus, you work together and walk together at the same time. That's when you will find your workday will become a lot easier. That was one of the hardest things in the world for me to learn, the transition from running to walking, and I'm still learning. I do not know why anybody would not want to take Jesus up on that promise. I'm glad I did many years ago and how sweet it is when you don't have all that stress in your life. That kind of rest can only come from Jesus like his joy we talked about. Here's the key Jesus says for that to happen: we have to do two things. First, we have to come to him; second, we have to learn about him, and the only way to do that is again read about him. This is another major benefit of why we need to take the time to learn about Jesus. I always like to say this: if Jesus is leading the way, then how can you have a bad day? In other words, don't work your schedule around God; let Him work His schedule around you. That's when you will find His true peace, rest, favor, and success. Take Jesus up on his offer by asking him each day to show you his yoke and learn about him and his easy ways. Although it took me most of my life to learn this, I believe anyone who starts practicing this can experience his rest and joy a lot sooner. The key is you have to stay connected to Jesus like the branch is to the vine and the yoke is to your neck. The hardest thing I learned about this is you can't rush and be in a hurry all the time. I used to drive my wife and family nuts with my always in a hurry, stressful ways. I had a bad habit of never allowing myself enough time and always jammed more things in one day to do than was even necessary. The first thing Jesus taught me about his rest and easy ways is I needed to slow down and allow enough time each day to put his yoke on. That's one thing Jesus made perfectly clear to me: he will not be rushed. Jesus wants to teach us how to enjoy the day with him, not rush it. There's no joy and rest in that. The simple solution is get up earlier. Jesus wants you to have the time to enjoy the things you need to do. Instead of rushing through it all putting stress on yourself, your family, and others. If that's you and the way you've been living, then that needs to change if you want to experience the joy and rest Jesus is talking about. Remember time is the most valuable gift you can give, and you are in control of how you spend it. I have learned when you choose to put God first by giving Him your time in every aspect of your life, He will show you the best way to spend it a lot better than we can.

Key questions to ask yourself:

• Are you seeking God's kingdom first or yours?

• Are you reading God's word and promises every day?

• How much time do you spend with God each day?

Key points to remember:

• Love God with all your heart, soul, mind and strength.

• Man shall not live by bread alone, but by every word that comes out of the mouth of God.

• Come close to God and he will come close to you.

God's promises to remember

• Seek ye first the kingdom of God and his righteousness,
and all these things shall be added unto you. (Matthew 6:33, KJV)

• I love them that love me, and those that seek
me early shall find me. (Proverbs 8:17, KJV)

• Come unto me all you who are weary and burdened and
I will give you rest. Take my yoke upon you, and learn
from me. For I am Gentle and humble in heart. And
you will find rest for your souls. (Matthew 11:28–29, NIV)

CHAPTER 7

THE SECOND STEP: TRUST IN GOD'S PLANS AND DIRECTION

O nce you have made the decision to put God first in every aspect of your life, the second most important step in God's priority's is putting your trust in God's plans and direction He has for your life. We already discussed that God created us with a purpose before the world even began. That means if He has a purpose, He also has plans for that purpose. In other words, you don't have to plan your life out: God has already done that. All we have to do is follow it. You might be saying, "How do you know what His plan is?" We don't know what His overall plan is. He shows it to us step by step and day by day putting our trust in Him. One of my favorite verses in the bible to support that is Proverbs 3:5, 6 KJV: "***Trust in the Lord with all thine heart, and lean not unto thine understanding. In all your ways acknowledge him and he shall direct thy paths.***" We are to trust Him with all of our plans. The hard part is not trying to figure it out. In other words, God has your whole life planned out for success with the talent and abilities he has given you to glorify him with. He has the right spouse, job, home, and where you're going to live already planned out and He promises to direct you to it all. Since I've been trusting the Lord with my plans, I don't have the stress and worry in my life like I did when I ran my own life. You might not think about it that way but it's the truth. In other words, stress and worry go hand and hand when we want to be in control of our life. That's because we want everything to work out according to our plan. And that doesn't always happen. That's what makes it so stressful, not knowing for sure what the outcome is going to be. On the other hand, the plans God has for your life are always going to work out as long as you follow them. When you trust God, you eliminate stress and worry because he's in control and not you. I believe there are many Christians who don't practice this second step. I think the main reason is they're not willing to trust God. The funny thing about it is we're willing to trust God for our salvation but why are we so reluctant to trust him with our life's plans? I think the answer to that is we want to be in control of that part of our life. Why is that? I think there's only one logical answer: we think we know what's best as we discussed earlier. The truth is when we're in control of our life, we actually miss out on God's best. It took me many years to realize that. We can make all the plans we want but if its not part of his will, it's not going to be a happy ending anyways. There may be some of you saying "If we can't make our own plans, then we might as well be a robot or puppet then." First of all, God never made a robot or puppet. Man did that so he could be in control of it without it making a choice. We are the only creatures on the planet that God made and allowed to make choices in their lives. So if you're someone thinking like that, look at it this way: if you have kids, you must know how they feel when they go into the store with you. In other words, they always have some kind of plan which is not part of your plan. They are going either to the candy or toy aisle to get something they want. Then they're going to beg you and try to get you to pay for it. Then you tell them no because it's not part of your plan today. That's when they start their plan B—to pout, fall down, kick and scream, or use another manipulative way they know. When that doesn't work, you make them follow you around that boring store watching you get what you want. That's got to be hard for a kid and it's hard for us as adults because we act the same way towards God. The problem is you and God can't be in control of your life's plans at the same time; that's a major conflict. That's like two people trying to steer the wheel at the same time: one wants to go one way and one wants to go another way. That's why there's one steering wheel, seat, and control panel for one person and who's that going to be—you or God? Another example if you got kids is when you plan a vacation, the goal is for everyone to have fun together. But what happens if your kids don't like your plan? Can they make their own plan, or do they have to follow yours? They have to follow your plans because you're the parent and they're not. The same way we are to follow God's plans because he's our father and creator were not. Just because we are adults doesn't give us the right to make our own plans according to our will, yet he allows us that choice. The point I'm trying to make is we act more like Him than what we think we do. God knows we want to be in control of our own destiny for success and happiness. As I said before, that is the only part of God He does not want us to copy. That is why He tells us to trust in him with all of our heart and all of our ways. When we do that, we give up our control to him. In other words, you can't play God and trust Him with your plans at the same time. It's one or the other; either you're the god of your life or he is the God of your life. He wants us to keep our trust in him on a daily basis, so he can lead us in the right direction he wants us to go. I used to trust in myself and make my own plans until the day I read Proverbs 28:26, NIV: **"Those who trust in themselves are fools."** The first thing I did after I read that was to find out what the bible's definition of fool is. In the bible, a fool means an arrogant self-sufficient person who plans their lives like there is no God. After I read that, it made me want to start practicing Proverbs 3:5, 6 and I've been doing it ever since. In other words, the bible says we are making one of two choices: trusting in our own heart and plans or trusting in God's. I remember how I felt in my early thirties before I knew what I know now. It was the most stressful time in my life. I always wanted to be successful; I just didn't know for sure what I wanted to do. That's because I didn't know God had a plan for me. I thought it was up to me to make my own plans and that's what made it so stressful. The bible says. *"A man's heart plans his way. But the Lord directs his steps."* (Proverbs 16:9, NKJV) Then it says if a man's steps are *"of the Lord;* **how then can a man understand his own way?"** (Proverbs 20:24, NKJV) In other words, even if a man makes his own plans, his steps are still directed by the Lord. So I said to myself, what's the point of making your own plans if God can override them anyway? If a man doesn't really know his own way, then what is the right way? The answer is back in Proverbs 3:5, 6 and John 14:6. If you believe that God has a purpose for your life but you don't know how to follow his plan each day, then that's what this second step is all about: fulfilling your purpose is to follow His plan. Years ago when I read the book *Purpose-Driven Life*, I realized God has a specific purpose for my life. The only problem I had about that is I didn't know what steps to take to find out what his purpose was. So I started asking God to show me what his purpose is; instead, he showed me these four steps and said, "Follow them each day and don't worry about purpose." For years that has been my question and still is, and only God knows the answer to that. God has a specific will, purpose, and plan for each of our lives. We find out what his purpose is as we go through life following his plan; that's where the trust factor comes in. Trust means having the belief, faith, confidence, and certainty that God has a better plan than we do. The danger comes when we make our own plans to do this or that. Because how do you know if it's His will or not? James 4:13–16 tells us what to do when we want to make our own plans. Some of you say, "Today or tomorrow we will go into such a city and stay there about a year, buy and sell and make a profit." How can you say that when you don't even know what tomorrow is going to bring? Ask yourself: is that what your life is all about? The truth is it's like a vapor that appears for a little time and then vanishes away. In other words, use the little time we have on earth wisely. This is what we ought to say, "If it's the Lord's will, we shall live here or do this or that." But when we rejoice about our own plans, all such boasting is evil. In other words, the key here is to make sure it is God's will and plan you're following and not your own. When you practice following His plan, He will always show you what's best. That's when things work out just perfect. I have learned the only time that doesn't happen is when you follow your own plan. There's nothing wrong with coming up with a plan; just make sure you're not dogmatic about it. In other words, allow enough room for God to change it and I can assure you it will always be for your best interest.

Why doesn't God show us the big picture?

When we trust God with our plans, He doesn't always show us the big picture. I believe that's because we couldn't comprehend or believe it if He did. Like when Joseph's brothers threw him in the pit: what if God told him then he was going to be the second most powerful richest person in the world. He wouldn't be able to comprehend it then because he was too far away from that destination for it to be believable. That's why God doesn't show us the whole picture in the beginning, because we're simply not ready yet. The only thing we can know for sure is he has a plan for us and we'll see it unfold as we trust him each day as we go through life. For example, I look at God's plan like putting together a puzzle without having the final picture to look at. All you know is you have a bunch of pieces that will fit together one piece at a time, like one day at a time. And the more pieces that you fit together, the more you will see what it's starting to look like. But it isn't until you finished that you can truly see the whole picture. I believe that's how God works his plan out in our lives: piece by piece day by day. That's why we have to keep our trust in Him. We are the pieces, God is the master builder, and when He is finished, we are His masterpiece that glorifies Him. Our life might be puzzling to us at times, but it never is to God. Even if God told us the whole plan He had for us, I think we might laugh and not believe it anyway. Like Abraham and Sarah did when God told them His plan ahead of time that he was going to be a father of a great nation when they were old and childless. When they heard that, the bible says they both fell down and laughed. Until almost twenty-five years later when God delivered His promise. The Bible says

Sarah laughed again; this time she wasn't laughing at God: she was laughing with him in belief. If God would have told me twenty-five years ago when I was in rehab that I would be writing a book about His steps on living a successful happy life, I know for sure I would have fallen down and laughed and not only me: my wife, my family, and all of my friends too.

I understand now why God doesn't show us His whole plan for us at once. I wasn't spiritually ready twenty-five years ago. I couldn't help myself, much less my family and others. I look at following God's plan like growing up: you can't hurry up the process. For example, when you were a baby, your mother had to feed you baby food because you didn't have teeth yet. You were not ready to chew and eat solid foods and meat. But it wasn't long before you started to get teeth and now you're feeding yourself and able to chew solid foods. Just like you had to crawl before you were able to walk. Your legs weren't strong enough to hold you up and you learned to walk before you could run. In other words, trusting God is like growing up step by step day to day and eventually we get there—that's how we follow his plan.

Are you following your dreams or God's plans?

This is the one thing that used to really bother me when I read Christian books about finding success and happiness. They would say things like follow your dreams and dream big because God is big. You can become whatever you want if you set your mind to it. Decide what you want to do, set a goal, make a plan, and follow it until you accomplish your dream. Can that way work? Yes, people do it all the time. Is there anything wrong with following your dreams? Only if it's your dream and plan and not God's; that's what you have to figure out. If you're asking, "How do I know if my dream or vision is from God?" If it's God's vision and plan, two things are for sure. One, it won't be anything contrary to His word. Two, it will be all about glorifying Him and His kingdom and not our own personal accomplishments. And I would say that part should be pretty easy to figure out. For example, God gave me a vision about writing this book. I didn't dream it up. I had other goals and plans I was pursuing for success in my business. That's when the Holy Spirit told me to stop what I was doing and gave me a new goal and plan to work on. In other words, from promoting myself and my business to promoting Jesus and God's kingdom business with two goals in mind. The first is to win as many souls to Jesus Christ as possible. The second is showing Christians how to live a true successful life by following Jesus' steps and plans he has for you. Based on that and the peace He has put in my heart, I know I'm following His purpose and plan to wherever that leads. And I believe that same principle of setting goals applies to all Christians. The key is making sure it's His goal and plan you're following and not yours if you want a successful outcome. Otherwise, down the road it will come to naught. I have been studying the bible for over twenty-five years; so far I have not found anywhere that God tells us to follow our dreams and make our own plans for success. But I did find in the bible where someone tried and that was Satan himself. That is where it all originated in the first place. God created him with a purpose and a plan just like He did with each of us, to glorify Him. The Bible says he was perfectly made full of wisdom and beauty in all his ways. He was a bright morning star and in charge of all the music and angels. His number one purpose and job was to lead the angels in praising and glorifying God. The bible tells us one day Satan got tired of being second place and wanted some of God's glory for himself. Satan was the first of his creation to rebel against God's authority, purpose, and glory. He spent way too much time looking in the mirror, dreaming big and thinking about his own goals and plans for what he wanted to be instead of what God created him for. Where do you think the world gets them same ideas? From none other than the prince of this world and originator of setting your own goal, Satan himself. Here is the danger when setting your own goals and plans: you start to believe in yourself instead of trusting God. Whenever we start trusting in ourselves is the same thing as Satan wanting to be like God. We might not look at it that way, but it's the truth and the way God sees it. When we trust in ourselves, we don't need God because we got our own goals and plans to accomplish. In other words, Satan wanted to go from being the star of God's show to being the star of his own show, where he gets all the glory. Listen to what he said when he was dreaming big about setting five goals outside of God's will. He said, "I will ascend into heaven. I will exalt my throne above the stars of God. I will sit in the mount of the congregation. I will ascend above the heights of the clouds." And his most famous line: "I will be like God." Those five words was Satan's downfall. The question is what can we learn from that so we don't make the same big mistake? Don't spend too much time looking in the mirror thinking about yourself and making goals outside of God's will. Instead, keep your focus on God. Make it your goal to follow His purpose and plan He has for your life. And always be satisfied with the way God created you and what He has given you. The bible says Satan was created perfect in all his ways except one day he became unsatisfied. He wanted what he couldn't have: some of God's glory and having His creation worship him. The problem with that kind of thinking is it will only get you in trouble. It surely won't lead you to a successful, happy life. God is allowing Satan what he wanted for now, but it won't be worth it in the end when his glory time is over. The same goes for us when we want to follow our own dreams and plans. One day, self-glory time is going to be all over, then what? We have all eternity to think about whether it was worth it or not. God is never going to share His throne or glory with anything he creates. God says, ***Everyone that is called by my name. For I have created him for my glory.*** (Isaiah 43:7, KJV) *He also* says, ***No flesh should glory in his presence.*** (I Corinthians 1:29, KJV) In other words, any glory we receive from others, we need to reflect it right back to God. He did not create us to absorb His glory. It is to shine through us for others to see and want to glorify Him. In heaven, there's only going to be one star of the show and that's going to be Jesus Christ in all his glory and we are part of that. God is not saying we can't have success and be a star as long as our light is shining on him. God has had the most successful stars in this world and they all glorified him. They were Noah, Abraham, Joseph, Moses, Joshua, and David just to name a few. The reason for their success was they trusted God and followed His plans and not theirs. He wants us to do the same thing. When God is behind it, nothing can stop you from reaching your destination for success except your own self. Not even the Devil can stop you unless you let him by listening to him tell you to follow your own dreams and plans and look where that got him. God's plan is for us to use the talents and abilities He gave us to shine like a star for His glory. Jesus says, "*Let your light so shine before men, that they may see your good works and glorify your father which is in heaven.*" (Matthew 5:16, KJV)

As Christians, that's our main purpose and reason for being here on earth. The first part of my life I thought and lived just the opposite: I always had to be in the limelight and the star of the show. Since then, God has shown me who really is the star. That's Jesus Christ our Lord and Savior, creator of all things who deserves all the praise and glory due his name.

God's plan A is always the perfect plan

I believe God has a plan A and B for all our lives. I'll explain the difference. His plan A is His perfect will that's to fulfill His purpose He created us for. His plan B is His permissive will, which allows us the freedom to make our own choices and plans that are not always part of His perfect will. In other words, His perfect will is for us to listen to Him and follow His plan just like what we want our children to do as parents. For example, our children are not always going to comply to our perfect will as we would like them to. I'll use the store analogy again because as parents I think we can all relate to that. Before we go into the store, we tell our kids what our plan and purpose is. Goes something like this: "We are not here to get toys or candy; we are here to get groceries. I want you to listen and mind me and stay right by my side." Then you tell them if they're good afterwards they can have a treat or reward of some kind. The same thing goes for us: we're not here just to please ourselves. We're here to fulfill God's purpose and will. And if we listen and follow His perfect plan, we will get rewarded too. When that happens, that's a perfect situation.

You're happy because your kids obeyed you by giving up their will and plan to obey yours. Your kids are happy because they got rewarded for it. Unfortunately, that perfect situation doesn't always work out that way. That's why you have plan B in case they choose to act up and not to obey your perfect will. Your plan B is usually some kind of consequence they will get for not following your perfect will. God deals with us the same way. For example, look what happened to King Saul. God told him His perfect plan and what He wanted him to do. But Saul deliberately chose to do his own plan his way which angered God. That resulted in his kingdom being taken away and his early death. Remember the bible says, *"Every way of a man is right in his own eyes."* (Proverbs 21:2, KJV) That's why we don't always see eye to eye because each of us think our way is right, especially between parents and their kids. Then whose way is right? God's ways are always right and perfect. I believe that's why God has his plan B because we can easily follow our own plans. In other words, his plan B is always to get us back to plan A, his perfect will. Jonah was a perfect example of that. He didn't want to follow God's plan A; instead, he rebelled with his own plan and went in the opposite direction. That's when God went to plan B and sent the whale until he came to his senses to go back to plan A. God's plan A is always the perfect plan because it always ends in success. It may not always look that way in the beginning, but it always ends that way. David realized that more than anybody. He said, "As for God, his ways are perfect." (Psalms 18:30) David learned as long he followed God's plan, he always had a perfect ending. God is the only one who can make a perfect plan work out every single time. Noah was an example of someone who followed God's perfect plan longer than anyone. Look how that turned out. I have to put a plug in here for Noah because I always thought he should have gotten more credit than he did for trusting God and sticking to his plan A. Put yourself in his shoes. Imagine you and your family are the only righteous people in the world who knew God and had a relationship with Him. Everyone else was living in wickedness doing what was right in their own eyes. Then God tells you about His plan that He is going to destroy all mankind and the earth with a flood. He tells you in every detail how to build an ark and gather in all the animals. And this goes on for 120 years. During this time, your neighbors and people are walking by your house asking you what you're building. So you tell them about God's plan and what He told you to do. We can't even imagine the kind of mockery Noah and his family must have had to go through day after day and year after year. People walking by hollering, "Hey, crazy Noah, when's that flood coming?" That had to be hard to listen to. But Noah stayed in faith and continued to trust in God's plan from the beginning to the end. We know the rest of the story: it ended just the way God planned it— perfect. When we make our own plans, things don't always work out the way we hoped or wanted it to. That's why we have plan A and B. A is our perfect plan when everything is supposed to work out the way we want it to. Our plan B is just our backup plan if plan A fails. I have always been a plan A and B person no matter what I'm going to do. As I said earlier in the book, that's why I didn't want to fly in a plane: I didn't believe it had a safe plan B. In other words, if the engine failed, you were going to crash and die unless God intervened with some kind of miracle. That's when my wife told me I wasn't really trusting in God's perfect plan. If I were, then I wouldn't need a plan B. She was right. That's when I started flying and trusting God more. On the other hand, I believe there are Christians who put more trust in a pilot they don't know to get them from point A to B than the God they do know. I have since learned that when you put all your trust in His perfect plan, you won't ever need a plan B because God's plan A never fails.

God's timing is always perfect

I believe in God's perfect will and plan there are no mistakes, accidents or coincidences; everything happens in perfect timing right down to the second. That's one of the benefits of living in his perfect will, knowing that everything is going to successfully work out. Sometimes God will show you things that you couldn't plan even if you wanted to. For example, here's a story in my life I won't ever forget.

A few years ago, we went on a cruise that was a last-minute deal. A few weeks before we left, we were talking to our best friends, telling them about it and what islands we were going to. One of them was Aruba. When I said that, my friend said they were going to Aruba too for a week. I said, "When are you going?" When he told me, I couldn't believe it was the same week and on the one day we were going to be there. So we ended up meeting them for that day and had a great time. We both knew that God was behind it because there is no way in the world we could have planned it to work out that way. Especially when we took a last-minute cruise and they had their vacation planned way before ours. Some people might call that a coincidence, but there's no way I'll ever believe it. That was part of his perfect will, plan, and timing to meet our best friends on vacation in another part of the world. When things happen like that, you can't help but be full of joy and thank Him for being an unbelievable cool God. I never look forward to any plan B. I always want the perfect plan to work and I think most of us do. And if that's the case, wouldn't it be a foolish thing not to want to follow God's perfect plan? Here's what I have learned about God's plan A and B. When we choose to follow his plan A, it always has rewards and benefits. It's a guaranteed perfect plan that always works out in His timing. The mistake we need to avoid is adding our plan B to his plan A when things aren't going according to our timetable like Abraham and Sarah did. God does not need our help to speed up His plan. He just wants our trust. On the other hand, His plan B has consequences that we cause upon ourselves when we don't follow His perfect plan A. I had to learn that the hard way, living many years of my life in his plan B. The nice thing about following God's plan A is He gives you an inner peace and joy which lets you know you're on the right track. This is whole lot better than the alternative of consequences we get reminding us we are on the wrong track. Remember no matter what plan you choose, God is always in control of the outcome. I have found it's a lot smoother sailing going with the wind than against it. I will admit it can be a little stressful at times when the storms pop up in your life without warning. To us it's a surprise; to God it's not because he's behind it—nothing happens without His approval. We also have to remember part of his plan is testing our faith. To be honest, that part I don't look forward to. On the other hand, it has to happen. It's the way God strengthens our faith. Like the miracle with my wife's brain tumor. If I didn't go through that, I wouldn't have the confidence and the story to tell that nothing is impossible with God. When you put your trust in God's plan, He will give you what you need when you need it at the right time all the time. And a lot of those times will come right down to the last second like when Peter was walking on the water to meet Jesus. At first he was successfully walking on the water until he took his eyes off Jesus and focused on the wind and waves around him. That's when he started to sink and cried out to Jesus, "Lord, save me!" And right at the last second before his head went under, Jesus reached out his hand and pulled him up and said, "Peter, what happened to your faith? Where did you not trust me?" When we take our eyes and trust off Jesus in our life, that's when we're going to sink. If you're in a situation where you feel like your life is sinking, do what Peter did: cry out to Jesus and ask him to save you and pull you up. And when he does, make sure to trust in him and follow him every day. Another example of trust is when God told Abraham to sacrifice his son as burnt offering. And right down to the last second before Abraham's arm came down with the knife to slay his son, the angel of the Lord said, "Stop! Don't lay your hand on the child. Now I know that you fear and trust God." That had to be one of the most terrifying and blessed moments of his life. Abraham passed the ultimate trust test. Now I see why he's called the father of faith. The bible is full of stories where God comes through right at the last second. That's why we need to keep our trust in Him right down to the last second if we want to pass the trust test. I call those times the testing of your faith when he comes right out of nowhere and bam, there's God's favor. The miracle you were hoping for, the right house you've been praying about, the job you so desperately needed, you found your perfect mate, you're finally pregnant with the child you thought you could never have, you got an unbelievable deal or blessed with something you never saw coming. When you trust and wait on God, you will always get His best, which always ends up better than what you could imagine. When you put all your trust in God, you're forfeiting your will and control of your life's plans. And that is not an easy thing for most Christians to do. Jesus himself even struggled with God's plan A and perfect will when it came right down to it. Listen to how he felt and prayed before he went to the cross.

"Father, if it's possible, let your plan A pass from me and do this another way. Nevertheless not as I will, but let your will be done." We should all praise Jesus for sticking to God's plan A and perfect will. And thank God for not giving Jesus his request, otherwise we'd have to pay for our sins. Jesus not only paid the price for our sins, but he also paid the price for our body, soul, and will. That being the case, don't we at the very least owe our will to Jesus then? He set the perfect example of how to surrender our will by sticking to God's plan A. That's where your faith comes in: you have to believe and trust God always has a better plan than you do. For us to think we can come up with a better plan than God is totally foolish. Remember without faith we can't please God and without trust it takes him longer to lead us to what's best for our life. It took the Israelites forty years to get to the Promised Land when it could have taken just eleven days. All because they didn't trust God. They were a stubborn and rebellious people. Without trust, it is like trying to lead a stubborn mule to where you want it to go. The key is to get the mule to trust you first, then he will follow you to your destination. Sometimes we can be like stubborn mules when it comes to putting our complete trust in God. The more you put your trust in God's plan A, the easier it is for him to lead you in the right direction.

Who's got your will, you or God?

To surrender our will to God is the most ultimate thing we can do as Christians to please him. The bible says, "*In him we were chosen, having been predestinated according to the plan of him who works out everything in conformity with his purpose of his will.*" (Ephesians 1:11, NIV) I believe God has two wills: his general will that applies to all of us which is to listen and obey all His commandments. Then there is his specific perfect will that is different for each of us, such as whom you're going to marry, how many children you're going to have, where you're going to live, and what you're going to do for a living. Then it gets even more specific; it's the spiritual gifts and talents that he gives each of us to glorify him with. The question I think most of us have is how do we know what God's specific will is? The short answer is trust him with your will and plans and be committed to following his four steps in this book. The long answer is going to be at the end of your life when you look back on the journey he has taken you. In other words, God's specific will and purpose for your life may not be any one lifelong thing; it may be several or many things. You don't have to strain your brain trying to figure that out, because that's God's part. In fact, God never once tells us to try to figure out what our purpose is. We do that daily by surrendering our will to him listening, trusting, and following his direction; that's the part God wants us to focus on. For example, I don't know what overall purpose God has planned for my life. In the meantime, I focus on the number one purpose he has already given most of us, our family's. Each day I work at trying to be a better godly husband, father, and grandfather than I was the day before. In other words, no matter what God has me do in the future from this point, it's not going to be as important of a purpose as that. I strongly believe there is no greater purpose and responsibility God has called us to do than to be a godly example of what he's truly really like, starting with our family first. If you're a parent, God gave you the greatest purpose and responsibility on the planet. Nothing should supersede that. God woke me up to that twenty-five years ago when I was an ungodly example of a person, husband, and father. That's where God had me start and I'm still working at it today and will be to the end. As far as I'm concerned, that is my main purpose. If I miss that, I've missed it all. Recently I had my sixty-second birthday and my daughter got me a card. She wrote, "Happy Birthday, Dad, and thank you for showing me Jesus is the way and because of that, Jesus is my best friend in the whole world." Those were the best words anyone has ever said to me in my entire life so far. I'm sharing that with you to point out if you're a parent, how can any purpose be more fulfilling to hear than that? And as great as it would be to hear that from a million other people, it is not the same as hearing it from your own child. If you're a parent, don't overlook your family: they are your first mission field.

God gave them to us to teach and show by example how great, loving, forgiving, and cool God really is. Start by asking yourself and your family: are you being a godly example to them? If yes, than praise the Lord because this world is in short demand of real godly parents. If your answer is no, then start working at it every day. What's holding you back from the greatest purpose in the world? I can tell you one thing: being a godly parent is God's number one priority over any other purposes he has for our life. This second step of trusting and surrendering your will to God can be a game breaker for many Christians. In other words, I believe a lot of Christians don't want to take this step and I was one of them for many years. That's because it's against our nature to surrender. We want to be in charge and in control of our destiny. "Surrender" is a battle term commonly used when we're defeated by the enemy, giving up our will to their authority. In fact, most people would rather die before giving up their will than to submit to another's. Like our forefathers said, "Give me liberty or give me death." In other words, unless we have the freedom to use our will the way we want to, we would rather be dead. That's why this is not an easy step to take; at least it wasn't for me. I trusted my plans to God first before I gave up my complete will. At that time, I wasn't ready to give up everything. I was still holding on to a few bad habits. Plus, I didn't know then what I do know now, so for me it was a gradual process. And I'm not suggesting that as the way to go either; that is entirely between you and God. Jesus said, "**Whoever does not take up their cross and follow me is not worthy of me.**" (Matthew 10:38, NIV) That's a pretty powerful statement. In other words, Jesus is saying we need to deny our self, our will and plans to him like he did for his father if we want to be a true follower. That's one verse that used to bother me the most every time I read it because I knew I wasn't doing it. And when I would stop and think about it for a few seconds of maybe taking that step, the Devil would pop in and say, "That's not for you. That's a boring way to live and you know you can't live that way." The Devil was right about me not wanting to live a boring life. He just lied about the denying myself and following Jesus part would be a boring life. Just in case the Devil might be telling you the same thing, the truth is it's the exact opposite of boring: for me, a surrendered life has been the most exciting and adventurous way I have ever lived. In other words, when you don't know what God's exact plan is next, that's what makes it adventurous. That's when you see his favor and blessing pop up everywhere in your life. Like when we met our friends in Aruba, God had that all planned out. That was exciting and adventurous. God had to be sitting back with a smile on his face. The other thing I learned is Jesus is far from being boring. The truth is if anybody's boring it's the Devil, because he gets you to do the same stupid stuff over and over again. Then he sits back and laughs while you pay the consequences and blame someone else. That's not only boring—it's stupid. Here's what I believe giving up your will to God is all about. First off, I don't look at it as being a sacrifice anymore. I look at it as being a privilege and honor. Our goal and first commandment is to love God with all our heart, soul, mind, and strength. In other words, we can't truly love God 100 percent in all those three areas until we completely surrender our will to him. What is our complete will? I believe it is part of our soul that dictates and controls what we do with our body. And in addition to that, it's our daily life divided up into three areas within the 24 hours God gives us. For example, most of us it's 8 hours of sleep, 8 hours of work, and 8 hours of free time, which equals 24 hours. How we spend the time in each of those areas is going to be different for each of us according to our will and plans. We all have the same 24 hours no more or no less to do what we want with. Our will is the freedom God gives us to dictate what we are going to do in each of those areas I call our complete will. When you surrender it all to Jesus, you don't have anything more to give. At first, that sounds like you will be left empty because you got nothing left for yourself. And there's some truth to that, because that's what carrying your cross and dying to yourself is all about. But here's the trade-off: when you surrender all to Jesus, he doesn't leave you empty and unsatisfied. If that was the case, none of us could live that way for very long. I know I couldn't. The truth is he fills you with his peace and joy, which is the only thing that truly satisfies your soul. When we get to the point of surrendering all the areas of our life to Jesus, I believe that's the time we are ready to do his specific perfect will. That's because we're not distracted by our own will, plans, and bad habits. I have lived my life both ways and mostly a partially surrendered life as I said and that's not the best way to live. Let me put it to you this way: if you're living a partially surrendered life, then you're only partially enjoying God and all his benefits. The sad part is you're the one who is really missing out.

Sin and demons go hand and hand

If you're a Christian who likes the idea about gradually giving up your will little by little instead of all at once, that's not the way I would recommend but it can work because I did it. The difference is it takes you longer to get there. I call it the longer way. But I must warn you there are a lot of problems and consequences with that way. In other words, sin and demons go hand and hand and if we gradually give up the sin in our life, then we gradually get rid of our demons. One thing is for sure: you can't get rid of your demons and still keep whatever sin is going on in your life. That doesn't work because God won't allow it plain and simple. I wasted at lot of years trying that. I'll tell you what does work: get rid of any sin you're practicing and you'll get rid of your demons. Whether you do that all at once or one sin at a time is totally up to you. And it depends on how fast you want to start enjoying Jesus' peace and joy in your life. You see, the demons do not like to hang around surrendered Christians who have Jesus' peace and joy in their life. That's because they can't deal with peace and joy; their purpose and mission is to destroy them. I learned if you don't have any sin you're practicing or holding on to, then they don't have an invitation. In other words, when we practice sin we're inviting them into our life. What it boils down to is how much of your will are you surrendering to the Devil and how much goes to Jesus? For example, let's look at it in percentages: the high number for Jesus and low for the Devil. Is it 50/50, 75/25, 90/10, 95/5, 99/1 100/0? In other words, what percentage of your life are you still holding on to that's not surrendered to Jesus? My point here is not about being perfect; it's about the sin you're practicing. Even if you're 99/1, meaning you only have one sin thing in your life you're holding onto that is not approved by God, you might be convincing yourself that's way better than the other percentages and I would agree with you as far as that goes. Because I lived a 99/1 for many years, convincing myself of that very same thing. To everybody else on the outside, you'll look like you're sold out to Jesus. The problem with that is what's happening spiritually to you on the inside. In other words, that one thing will keep you from having total peace in your life.

The battle of wills

As long as we hold on to things in our life we know God doesn't approve of, there's going to be battles going on. Any area of your life that is not committed to God, the Devil has access to. That's why he wants us to surrender all to him. In other words, here's the deal: there's God's will, there's the Devil's will, and there's you and your will, and that's the battle. That means as long as you keep some of your will to yourself, God and the Devil are going to be battling over it because they both want it. As Christians, we need to wake up and realize we are in a battle every day, especially those who have not fully surrendered their will and life to God. Every day we wake up to a spiritual battlefield, not a playground as it may seem. We may want to play but God and the Devil don't. They are in a serious battle against each other 24/7 for one thing: your will. The apostle Paul warns us of that and tells us we need to be strong in the Lord and the power of His might—by putting on all of the armor of God so we can protect ourselves against the deceit and trickery of the Devil. The real battle isn't against flesh and blood, it's against the prince of this world, Satan and his demons. (Ephesians 6:10–17) It wasn't until God opened my eyes up to this battle that I made up my mind to give up my bad habits and commit all my will to Him. I didn't go around thinking God and the Devil are fighting over my will or that there was any harm keeping it to myself. Until one day I was praying asking God to get rid of the demons in my life and the Holy Spirt said to me I needed to surrender my complete will to him first. I said, "What?" I thought I did years ago. I was putting God first reading his word, committing my plans, and following his direction. That's when the Holy Spirit pointed out the one bad habit I'd been holding on to for many years. He said, "You need to stop that first" and He said that more than once, which scared me a little bit. Right then I knew that was God talking because it surely wasn't me. That was the day I completely gave up the last thing the Devil was holding me captive to. When your will is completely sold out to God, it means there's no seats left for the Devil in your life. God wants you to surrender your complete will to him so he can fulfill his perfect will in you for his glory. The Devil wants your will so he can cause chaos in your life, so you can't glorify God. That's what the spiritual battle is all about and will continue until you decide to end it. How do you end it? Like you would in any battle, put up the white flag. The only difference is you're not surrendering to the enemy who keeps you captive from your freedom to enjoy happiness. Instead it's just the opposite: you're surrendering to Jesus the King of Kings Lord of Lords. The one who died to set you free from being captive, so you can have peace, joy, and happiness.

Jesus is our perfect example to follow. He said, "I'm not here to seek my own will but the will of my father who sent me. Therefore, that's how my father is glorified. We're supposed to do the same thing. We're not here to fulfill our own will; we're here to fulfill His. David was another good example. God said, "*I have found David the son of Jesse, a man after my own heart, who will do all my will.*" (Acts 13:22, NKJV) On the other hand, your enemy the Devil, the world, and maybe some of your friends are going to tell you the opposite—that surrendering your will and plans to God is not a happy way to live. The Devil will try to convince you to doubt God, that you can't be happy by surrendering all your will to him. Then he reminds you of the things you're doing that God doesn't approve of. Then he whispers things like this in your ear, "Do you really want to give that up? Think about how much you like it and how fun it is. Do you really want to surrender all of that? You need to keep at least a few things for yourself, so you can be happy. Maybe take a little more time and think about it first." The reason I know those lies is I used to listen to them way too much for way too long. Here's what I recommend I call the shorter way: the sooner you commit all your will and plans to God, the sooner it will be when you have God's peace, joy, happiness, and direction in your life instead of the Devil's chaos and turmoil.

Whose team are you on?

Another thing I learned is you can't be a free agent Christian with your will either. In other words, you can't be neutral; you're either on God's team or default to the Devil's. When I wasn't fully committed to God, I defaulted to the Devil's team without realizing it. We can't play on both teams: it's one or the other. We can't be on God's team one day and the Devil's the next and expect to live a peaceful happy successful life. I tried that angle, the free agent lifestyle: that doesn't work with God. Here's the way that does work and Jesus makes it perfectly clear when he said, "**He that is not with me is against me.**" (Matthew 12:30, KJV) In other words, Jesus is not allowing us to be free agents with our will. He's saying we have to make a choice: we're either on his team or not. Jesus came here to do God's will. If we want to be on his team, we need to do the same thing. Jesus knows when we're not fully committed to him, we become vulnerable to the schemes and tricks of the Devil. That's why the bible says, "**We are to be alert and of a sober mind.**" *Your enemy the Devil prowls around like a roaring lion looking for someone to devour.* (I Peter 5:8, NIV) In other words, the Devil is like the lion and the lion is the king of the jungle. And even though he is the top of the food chain, he is always stalking for the weakest prey because it's the easiest. He doesn't waste his time and energy going after the strongest and the fastest; he hunts and waits for the weak and vulnerable. That's the same thing the Devil does to us: he's hunting for Christians who are weak and vulnerable, who have not fully committed their will to God. The bible says the Devil sets snares and traps so he can take us captive at his will. (II Timothy 2:26, KJV) Don't forget the Devil has a will and plans too, which is to take us hostage at his will. He wants to keep us captive in our sin so we won't surrender our will to God. If you know the Lord as your personal savior the Devil can no longer get your soul. But he does have access to your will if you let him. I believe the Devil has a plan A and B just like God does; that's where he got it from. His plan A is to get as many people to follow him to hell as possible. His plan B is to get as many vulnerable Christians who haven't committed their will to God as possible, to make their lives a miserable hell on his road to destruction if you let him. Christians who have committed their will and plans to God have protection and advantage over the Devil. The Devil can't take them captive at his will anymore when it's all committed to God. As long as your will stays committed to God, the Devil can't get it without your permission. If you're a Christian and you have never surrendered your will and plans to God, I would encourage you to make that decision. The longer you wait, the longer you'll be missing out on God's best plan for your life. It's also the quickest way to get the Devil off your back and his demons out of your life. You'll sleep better at night and wake up each day with peace and joy, knowing you're committed to following God's will and perfect plan. That's what the Devil wants to keep you from. Don't let the enemy of the cross have any more victories in your life. Let Jesus have the victory. He's the one who died for you, who rightly deserves your will. Jesus is the only one you can surrender to that there is no shame or defeat. Instead, you experience the victory of peace, joy, and happiness because the battle of your will is over; now, you're on the winning team. Why wait any longer for that? Take the next step by surrendering all your will to him today. Then start your day like David did. He said, "Cause me to hear your voice oh Lord in the morning, I put all my trust in you show me the way I should walk today and teach me to know your will." (Psalms 143: 8, 10) In my opinion, that is a daily model prayer that every Christian should be asking God for.

Key questions:

• Are you trusting God with all your heart for his direction in your life?

• Have you surrendered your will in every area of your life?

• Are you following your dreams or Gods plan?

Key points to remember:

• He that trust in his own heart is a fool.

• God has predestinated us for a purpose according to his own will.

• Jesus said he that is not with me is against Me.

God's promises to remember:

• Trust in the lord with all thine heart, and lean not unto thine own understanding. In all your ways acknowledge him, and he shall direct thy paths. (Proverbs 3:5, 6, KJV)

• As for God his way is perfect. (Psalms 18:30, NIV)

• Show me the way I should go, for to you I entrust my life. Teach me to do your will for you are my God. (Psalms 143:8, 10, NIV)

CHAPTER 8

THE THIRD STEP:
COMMIT ALL YOUR WORK
UNTO THE LORD

Once I trusted God with my will and plans, I started asking him, "What do you want me to do next?" In other words, how do we know what God's will is and how do we follow his plan, so we know we're on the right path? That was my question before God showed me this third step. I was expecting to get some kind of vision or something, but that never happened. As I said earlier, God doesn't show us his plan all at once. When I got to this point in my life, I didn't know what to do next other than what God was showing me through studying his word. I didn't realize it as I do now that God was showing me step by step in priority how to live each day according to his will. Then one day I was reading in Proverbs. That's when he revealed this third step to me: *"Commit your works to the Lord and your thoughts will be established."* (Proverbs 16:3, NKJV) After I read that, I had another turning point in my life. I was excited. It was like finding gold. I said, "This has to be it, the next step after you trust God with your will and plans." When we commit our work to the Lord, He tells us what to do next by directing our thoughts. The first question is what is our work? Our work is anything that we labor to do with our hands, mouth, and mind to help others and glorify God with such as the special gifts, talents, and abilities he created us with. The bible says, "*We are God's handiwork, created in Jesus Christ to do good works.* **Which God prepared in advance for us to do***.*" (Ephesians 2:10, NIV)

In other words, we are uniquely designed for the purpose of doing good works. "Prepared in advance" means we are already equipped with the necessary spiritual gifts and talents to do those good works. There may be some of you who already know what your talents are. The question is are you using them for the glory of God and does He get the credit? There may be some of you who don't think you have any talent. Because you may look at talent like being a singer, musician, dancer, or something like that. You don't have to be on stage or in the limelight to have talent. In other words, talent is simply having a unique ability of doing something that no one else in the world can do quite like you. God also created each of us with one or more spiritual gifts to help others with. Read I Corinthians chapter 12: that tells about all the different spiritual gifts. The apostle Paul tells us every believer who is a member of Christ's body has a assignment of work to do in the ministry with the gifts God gives them. In other words, we are all ministers of Christ and no one is exempt from that. If you don't know what your gift or assignment is yet, start asking him to show you, because he doesn't want it to be a secret. The bible tells us God took the time to make each of us special and unique from anyone else in the world for the purpose of helping others to know Christ more. In other words, when God made you, he threw the mold away. That means no one else can be what you were created to do; that's how much responsibility you have. Some of us might look alike, walk alike, and talk alike, but not one of us is exactly alike, not even twins. That's one of the interesting and unique characteristics of God: he doesn't create anything the exact same. Everything that God creates has its own purpose that is different and unique from all others of its kind.

How committed are you?

If you're not sure what your gifts and talents are right now, that's okay. What matters most is being committed to finding out what they are. In the second step, we learned that God wants us to trust in his plan for our whole life. Since he doesn't show us his whole plan all at once means it is broken down to daily assignments of what he wants us to do. I believe God's first assignment is for us all to get a good night's sleep—for example, 8 hours. God's ultimate commandment is to love him with all our heart, soul, mind, and strength. That means we need to have the right amount of sleep so we can be our best at his assignments for the day, which is about 16 hours. In other words, it's hard to give God your best if you're tired and run down all the time. And I don't believe He wants us to live like that. Jesus certainly didn't live that way. He made sure he got his rest. Let me explain what I mean about assignments. I believe we all have daily assignments from God. Those can be many things: a job, duty, chores, errands, tasks, projects, volunteer work, etc. In other words, God has assignments for us each day to accomplish His will and plan to do our work in. It would be foolish to think He has a plan without steps and assignments with it. For example, Noah was committed to following God's assignments every single day till his overall plan was finished. I believe God wants us to do the very same thing Noah did. Wake up every day committing your work to following God's assignment and plan he has for you whatever that is. The key here in the third step is not to overlook the word "commit." I think it is vitally important to understand the full gravity of the word first. Commitment is loyalty, dedication, and faithfulness of our actions that speak louder than words. Commitment is not based on our circumstances or conditions. It is an unconditional choice we make and promise to stick to day after day and year after year. It makes time when there is none. It shows what real character is made of. It has the power to change the face of things, and finally it transforms God's promises into reality. One thing is for sure: God has showed us first the kind of commitment we should have toward him by sending his son Jesus Christ to die on that cross to be our Lord, Savior, and example. The question is are you willing to show that same kind of commitment back to Him? This is the same kind of commitment we make in our wedding vows to our mate. All successful marriages that last the test of time are based on that one-word commitment. The same goes with God if you want a successful, joyful life with Him. He requires nothing less. If you're married, God requires you to have a more committed intimate relationship with him than your spouse. That's one way of knowing how close of a relationship you have with God if you're married. Ask yourself this question: do you know more about God or your spouse? Who do you talk more with each day, God or your spouse? The goal and the answer should always be God. I've been married and committed to my wife for over forty-two years and I'd have to say the first twenty-five of those years I had a more intimate relationship with her than I did with God. That's because I didn't know how to until He started showing me these four steps, especially this third one. In other words, regardless of how long you have been married, the goal should be to have a closer relationship with God than your spouse or anyone. If you can't say that right now, then you got a lot of exciting things to look forward to. When you start practicing this third step about commitment, you'll wish you started sooner. That's because God's got a lot more things to show you in terms of benefits than your spouse, that's why we should be communicating with Him more. He's the one who is the source of all our benefits, including our spouses. In other words, one way you know you're truly committed to God is when you're communicating to Him more than anyone else in your life. God does not take commitment lightly. He commands us to be 100 percent committed to Him and our spouse. I have learned that if you're not 100 percent committed to God's plan every day, you're going to miss out on His best. For example, God's plan for the children of Israel was to enter into the promised land of milk, honey, and prosperity. He had the whole plan laid out with guaranteed success. All they had to do was follow his plan. But the majority of them were afraid and didn't want to commit their trust to His plan. And look what happened: they all missed out on God's best because they wouldn't commit to His plan. Except for Joshua and Caleb, they were the only ones out of that group who did trust and commit. Therefore they got to experience the promise of prosperity and God's best. I believe that same example and principle applies to us today. God has a plan for each of us and that plan is to be successful. God said, "*I know the plans I have for you, declares the Lord, plans to prosper you and not to harm you, plans to give you hope and a future.*" (Jeremiah 29:11, NIV) On the other hand, if we are not committed to His plan, we're going to miss out on His best just like the Israelites did. God wants us to commit our work into His hands every single day because He has assignments and a plan for us to accomplish according to His will. Once you have decided to commit your work and whatever it is you do into God's hands, He promises to direct your thoughts. In other words, God always expects us to do our part first before He does His. If you have never done this before, then put God to the test. Start out each day by telling Him, "Lord, I'm committing my work into your hands. Direct my thoughts and footsteps. Show me all what I need to see, hear, and do today." I've been praying that every day for over twenty-five years now. If you commit to practicing that, I can assure you that you'll see God's plan unfold in every aspect and detail of your life. That's because when you're committed to God like that, you're mentally and spiritually ready for what's next in His plan.

God will direct your thoughts

I remember years ago when I first read that verse, "Commit your work unto the Lord and he will direct your thoughts." At first I thought that was a little strange. It was all new to me. I never heard that before by anyone, to be honest. I couldn't even comprehend it at that time. That's because back then, I didn't know how to listen to God. Basically I did all the talking. The biggest thing for me was trying to figure out what the differences between my thoughts and God's thoughts were. That took me quite a while and lots of practice to figure that out. But it all started with me doing my part first, committing all my daily tasks into God's hands.

Now I have many years of experience and examples of how that works. The primary way God communicates to us is through His word the Holy Spirit and directing our thoughts. I will tell you this step was the hardest thing in the world I have ever done. The reason is if God is going to speak to you in your thoughts, how do you listen while you're busy thinking of other things? That can be very difficult because it requires extraordinary listening skills. That's because he doesn't speak to us in an audible voice. And that was a big problem for me because according to my wife I was the worst listener in the world. We'll talk more about that in the fourth step. On top of that, she says I talk too much. In other words, I was the worst-case example of someone learning how to listen to God; if I can do it, anyone can. This was the step that showed me how to start listening. The key was being committed to it and for me that was the easy part. Commitment for me is my strong asset, as opposed to listening which is my weakest. In other words, my commitment to finding out how God directed my thoughts is what got me to listen to him more each day. I believe when people are committed to doing something, then they're ready to really listen. When God speaks to us in a still small voice, I have learned the only way you can hear it is you have to be quite with your thoughts. The bible says, *"Be still and know that I am God."* (Psalms 46:10, KJV) In other words, God is telling us we need to have quiet times in our life, where it is just you and God alone. During those times, I have found that He may speak to you about something or maybe not at all. The point is He wants us to stop what we're doing and acknowledge who He is and His presence during that time. For example, have you ever had a lover where the two of you wanted to get away and just be alone? Somewhere quiet from the distractions of this world so you could acknowledge each other's presence in private just you two? Or maybe you thought it was just you two but God was there all the time. That kind of private intimacy is the same thing God wants us to have with Him. The only difference is it's more intimate; in other words, one less person is one less distraction from God. I'm not saying that you both can't enjoy His presence together. It's just not the same experience as being alone because you're focused more on each other. I remember when we were raising our children, my wife and I made it a practice every six month to get away for a weekend somewhere just by ourselves. We did that so we could have a little time of peace and quietness together without the distractions of our kids. And it was just enough time to restore our sanity back to endure for another six months. In other words, just like we need peace and quiet time away from our kids, we need to have that same kind of time with God alone. And you don't have to wait six months to do that. You can do that every day if you choose to. If you have never done that, I would highly encourage you to at least try it. The key is no distractions, no smart phone, no music, no nothing, except you, God, and quietness. Find a place or places where you can do that. For me it's my hammock or when I go for walks by myself. And then I look and listen to all God's creation around me, at the same time acknowledging his presence. I remember when I first started to do that. It was a little spooky at first. What I mean is you are purposely setting out time to be quiet, shutting out your thoughts and any distractions for a few moments just to acknowledge God. It's those times when you tune in and realize you are in the presence of the almighty creator of all the things around you. It can be a hard thing to do if you don't purposely set your mind to it. That's where the commitment comes in. After I started doing that for a while, I asked my wife to try it. She didn't really want to. She thought it was stupid and a waste of time. I keep insisting that she try it at least once. She finally agreed but only for 5 minutes and plus I had to set the timer. So she's out on the patio, I was in the house. I heard her voice through the window asking me if the 5 minutes were up yet. I said, "No, it's only been 3 minutes." The thing I learned from that is it was uncomfortable for her to relax in quietness for even 3 minutes. In other words, if you allow yourself to be busy and distracted all the time like my wife was back then, you will be missing out on learning how to relax and walk in the quietness of the presence of the Lord. In my opinion, if you miss out on that experience, you're missing out on everything else. In other words, the key is when we are aware of his presence, we enjoy God in everything else. If this is something you have never done before, the first few times can be quite uncomfortable. For some people it is, as it was for me and my wife. Nowadays my wife looks for every opportunity to do that. The only difference is I don't have to set the timer. And sometimes we fight over who's going to get the hammock first and she tells me to be quiet a lot more. The funny thing about the hammock is my wife bought it for me for Father's Day over ten years ago to relax in. The first five years, I only used it two to three times. That's because I was too busy to know how to relax. Now it's the most relaxing thing I do. I remember when I first started telling my wife things about how God directed my thoughts to do this or that. She asked me, "How do you know the difference between what's your thoughts and God's thoughts?" It was the same question I had and I think everyone must have too. The general answer to that is God's thoughts are always going to be helping you in some way that you know you didn't think about. Otherwise if you have thought about it, you would have done it. For example, for me the biggest thing is I misplace and lose things a lot. This was one of the areas where I first started testing God to see if he really directs your thoughts. Helping me find things I've lost, misplaced, or things I already had that I didn't know I had. For example, one Sunday morning I had my tithe envelope ready on the kitchen counter the same place I always put it so I wouldn't forget it. And just before we were ready to leave for church, I went to grab the tithe envelope and it wasn't there. So I asked my wife, "Did you do something with the tithe envelope?" She said no. I said, "It was sitting right here on the counter a few minutes ago," while backtracking and looking all over the house thinking I might have set it somewhere else. I looked frantically over every square foot three or four times over and I still didn't find it. I couldn't believe it when it was just sitting there a few minutes ago on the counter. Time was running out; either we go to church without it or I look for it later. At that point I calmed down and said, "God, I give up. I know you know where it is. You see that I can't find it, please show me where it is." We have a trash can right next to the counter where the tithe envelope was. The next thing I know, I was looking in the trash can and I said to myself, "Why am I looking in here?" So I was digging through the trash.

My wife saw me and said, "What are you doing?" I said, "I don't know," and as soon as I said that, I couldn't believe it: there was the tithe envelope. Then I realized what happened: I grabbed some old newspapers to throw away and my tithe was in my hand when I thought I set it on the counter. It went into the trash can with the papers. How did I know that was God directing my thought? Because I already exhausted all of my thoughts and knew the trash can would have been the last place in the world I would think to look. It wasn't until I gave up thinking and asked God to show me where it was that I finally found it. That's how you know the difference between your thoughts and God's, when you know for sure it was Him who was behind it and not you. Another example I won't ever forget is when one night I was burning some scrap wood in my fire pit in my backyard. It was getting late. The fire was dying down so I took the garden hose and sprayed the fire out and all around beyond the fire because I have woods along my backyard. I thought I really saturated that fire with water too, where you couldn't see any more smoke. I even checked it several times again before I went to bed. Everything looked okay. Then I was awakened by a voice in my head that keep telling me to get up and I couldn't figure out why. I thought I was just dreaming. I opened my eyes to look at the alarm clock to see what time it was. I could see something glowing out of our bedroom window so I got up to see what it was. When I looked out the window, part of the woods was on fire. I couldn't believe it. The first words out of my mouth was, "Oh God no!" I felt like I said that a hundred times. It was about 2:00 a.m. The fire was so big I didn't think I was going to put it out with the hose. I just keep saying, "God, please help me." It took me about an hour to get the fire completely out. If it had been a few minutes longer, I would have had to call the fire department. I thanked God many times that day for getting me up just in time to get the fire out myself, which could have been a disaster. He showed me He's on duty 24/7 directing your thoughts even while you're sleeping. There is no alarm system in the world that could have helped me that day other than God himself. There was another big benefit I enjoy about God directing your thoughts and this is one of my favorites. He can find you the best deals on things and whatever it is you need. Whether you need a place to live, a car, an appliance, a vacation no matter what it is, one thing is for sure: God knows where all the deals are if you're willing to ask, be patient, and wait on Him, He will guide you to it. The area I practice this most is when I go shopping by myself. It's peaceful even though there are other people in the store. I feel like it's just me and God. I call it my shopping with God time. I've tried shopping with my wife and God and it's just not the same peaceful experience. Some of you might know what I mean. I'm always looking for the best deals; on the other hand, my wife doesn't care about a deal like I do. She just grabs and gets what she wants regardless of there being a deal or a sale. That's why we don't shop together. In other words, it's doesn't end up being a peaceful experience. Here's the deal: before I go shopping, I always have a list of everything that we need I can think of. I always ask God as I enter the store to direct my thoughts and show me if there is anything I need that I don't have on my list. The reason I say that is God says he knows what we need before we even ask, so I decided to take Him up on it when I go shopping. In other words, there can be something in the store that I need that I forgot to write on my list. Since I've been doing that, He has directed my thoughts to hundreds of things I needed that I forgot about. There have been many times I finished shopping and at the last minute, God directed my thought and said, "You need to go back down a certain aisle. And here's the funny thing: when I hear that little voice tell me, then I question it and say, "What for, I've already been down that aisle." In my mind there's nothing there I needed because I had what's on my list. But what I have learned through experience is listen to that voice or thought; anyways, don't try to make sense out of it or second-guess it. Just like when he told me to look in the trash can for my tithe, it made no sense at the time until afterwards. You just learn to listen and obey that voice, so I went down the aisle not knowing what I was looking for. And then bam, there it is! I see something that I needed a while ago but I forgot to put it back on my list. And the best part is it was on sale, so that's how I know it was God directing my thoughts—it wasn't on my list or on my mind.

That's why I enjoy shopping more with God than with my wife: He saves me money; she cost me money. I highly recommend making this part of your prayer request before you start your day to do anything. For the mere fact that you don't miss out on God's best, remember He knows where everything is and what we need before we do. Every day, ask God to direct your thoughts on what you need to see, hear or do, and make it a commitment—that is key. When you practice that every day, you will have all your bases covered. In other words, whatever it is you need to see, hear, or do, God will either speak to you in his still small voice or direct your thoughts to it.

In case you're wondering what's the difference between hearing His nonaudible voice and sensing Him direct your thoughts: the answer is you will hear His little quite voice but when He directs your thought, you don't hear anything. That's because God controls your thought to help you see or find something he wants you to. Sometimes God will do both at the same time: using his voice and directing your thoughts to help you see, find, or do something. This takes a lot of discipline and practice as it becomes a habit and part of your daily life. I can assure you as you practice, you will see more and more of God's favor show up in every aspect of your life. And when you see it happen, you'll' be so excited you can't wait to share that experience with someone. The only problem is having someone to share it with, someone who really believes it or understands you other than God himself.

God will teach you how to profit

When you commit your work to God, He promises to teach you how to profit. The bible says, "*I am the Lord your God, who teaches you to profit, who leads you by the way you should go.*" (Isaiah 48:17, NKJV) In other words, God has a job for you and not just any odd job. I'm talking about a job that's best for you that you will enjoy. You could be in a situation right now wherein you have a job that you hate or perhaps you don't even have a job, much less enjoy one. I understand: I've been in that situation before and I hated it too as I mentioned earlier in the book. If you're in that situation right now, you don't have to stay there. God may have us pass through the desert but that's not where he wants us to stay. In other words, I believe that when you're committed to following God's plan every day, He will give you the job that's best for you until He wants you to move on to a better job. Your part is to daily commit your work, plans, and thoughts into His hands and ask Him to lead you to the job that is best for you. Then get ready: it's going to happen. It's not a matter of if; it's a matter of when, but you must be patient and wait on God's timing. I know that because it has happened to me, my entire life, my wife, and my children. God has the perfect job for you. He created you and knows what you like more than what you do as we already discussed earlier. Plus, He promises to be your teacher, showing you the best way to profit in whatever way that is. If you're stuck in a job right now that you don't like, then that's not God's best—He's got something better. If you want God's best, take Him up on His promise and in His timing. You will see it come to pass. But here's the key: if you want God to teach you and show you how to profit, then you need to show up for class each day. In other words, God expects you to be committed and present each day so He can teach you in the way you should go. How can He teach you if you're not committed? God always expects faith, commitment, and consistency on our part. The bible says, "**When you ask you must believe and not doubt,** *because the one who doubts is like the wave of the sea, blown and tossed by the wind. That person should not expect to receive anything from the Lord.* **Such a person is a double minded man and unstable in all they do.**" (James 1:6–8, NIV) In other words, if you want to see God's best, you need to have three things: faith, commitment, and patience. And when it comes to patience, a lot of people don't want to wait on God. They want it right now. God doesn't work that way. He always does things on His timetable, not ours, and this is where a lot of people will get off the train. Sorry to say, but those who don't have the patience to wait on God will miss out on His best. Sometimes we have to go through the desert and the wilderness to get to the Promised Land. Our part is to make sure we stay in faith and be committed to following His instructions. For example, my wife had three different jobs that she worked at about ten years each. The first job she worked for was the same company chain that I worked for. In the beginning she really enjoyed her job like I did, but towards the end she started to dislike it. That's because her boss that she liked retired and her new boss made her job so miserable that she quit. Then God blessed her with a better job than the one she had, and it turned out to be a perfect situation. A friend of hers just bought a little party store just around the corner from our house and hired her to help run it. It was the perfect job: she liked her boss, her hours, her pay, everything about it, plus she could have walked to work if she wanted to. Then after ten years, her boss got tired of running the hundred-year-old store and decided to have it torn down and built her house there. That was sad news to hear for us because it was the end of a perfect job situation. At the time, I didn't see how it could get any better than that. And at about the same time they were tearing down the old store, a new restaurant was opening up right across the street. They were hiring waitresses and she got the job right around the corner from our house again and worked there for ten years. In the beginning, she really enjoyed her new job: perfect hours, and she liked her boss. Then the last few years her boss started taking advantage of her, making her do different jobs with no increase of pay. She felt like she was being taken advantage of. She couldn't take it anymore. She would come home all upset, so I told she didn't need that anymore, that God's got something better for her. She quit and took off about a year before she started looking for work again. That's when she started to realize how blessed and spoiled she was for about twenty years. Not many people get to work right around the corner from their house, especially for that long. I asked her, "What type of job do you want to do now?" She didn't really know, so she started praying about it and applying for jobs that were closest to our house. I told her, "God's got the perfect job already picked out for you. Your part is to keep praying and seeking and he will guide you to it." She worked three different jobs in one year, trying to find the perfect job she really liked. My wife came home one day and said to me, "Why is God doing this to me, putting me through more jobs in one year than she had in thirty years." I didn't have an answer. I was getting a little discouraged too. I know He has a reason but I just don't know what it is. I said, "Just keep believing God knows what He's doing. He's going to get you the job that's best for you." I added, "Just look back on what he has already done for you. He did it before, He can do it again." That same week, my wife got a call from her sister and said there's an opening for a job where she worked that my wife should check out. She applied and got the job. She told me her boss is the nicest guy in the world. In fact, he told her she can come in when she wants, leave when she wants, and work when she wants. All she has to do is let him know ahead of time. When she first told me that, I said, "You have to be kidding me. No one gets to do that. It sounded too good to be true. How come people aren't standing in line to get that job?" Come to find out no one knew about it because it was a new position. She was first to apply and first to get the job. So far she has said this last job is the best all-around job she has had in her life. The boss, the hours, the pay, the flexibility—it's the perfect job again. I believe that God has the perfect job for all of us when we commit our work to Him. Sometimes we might have to go through some adversity to get there because God is trying to teach us something or He wants us to move on to something better. There is something I learned most about adversity with bosses in my wife's and my work history as we look back on them now. I thank God for allowing our bosses to be jerks. If it weren't for them making our life miserable and unhappy, we might still be there. Our first natural reaction is to take it personally, especially if you're not doing any-thing wrong at all like with Joseph, and look at how he ended up. You might have to go through some adversity to get to the Promised Land but if you stay in faith, God will get you there no matter what because He always keeps His promises. My wife asked me why God didn't give her the job she has now right off the bat. I said I don't know the answer to that but if I had to guess, it would be because if God gave us the best right when we asked, we could easily take things for granted and not need as much faith and without faith, you can't please God. Maybe you're in that situation like my wife: you started out in a job you liked and enjoyed and through the years, things have changed for the worse. Whether it's your boss, your hours, your pay, your benefits or flexibility and you're not happy about it, don't take it personally. It could be God allowing adversity to happen because He has bigger and better plans for you. We should never lose this perspective that Jesus is the one we get up for and go to work for each day. He's the one who meets all our needs, not our boss or the company we work for. The bible teaches us we are to be obedient servants to those who that have authority over us, and yes, even if they happen to be a jerk. And at the same time we are to be servants of Jesus doing the will of God. (Ephesians 6:5, 6, KJV) In other words, no matter what your job is or who you're helping. The bible says, "**Whatever you do, work at it with all your heart, as working for the Lord, not for human masters, since you know that you will receive an inheritance from the Lord as a reward. It is the lord Christ you are serving.**" (Colossians 3:23, 24, NIV) When we get up each morning, we should have the mind-set that we're serving Jesus today. He will never let you down and nothing you do ever gets unnoticed or overlooked. He rewards us justly both here on earth and in heaven. You don't have to be concerned about recognition. He's always watching when no one else is, and his records are always accurate. Even if things look hopeless for you right now and you don't see anything good happening on the horizon, the key is to stay in faith: he might just be testing you and don't worry about God's part, how and when it's going to happen. Just do your part by trusting and committing your work unto God on a daily basis. That's what He expects us to do. And when you stay committed to Him, I can assure you that's when you'll see His promises become reality, always leading you to a better place or situation.

Key questions:

• Do you commit your work unto the Lord?

• Do you ask God to direct your thoughts before you start each day?

• How committed to Jesus are you?

Key points to remember:

• When you're committed to following God's plan, things always work out for the best.

• When your mind is distracted all the time, it's hard to hear His voice.

• Make more quiet times in your life, where it's just you and God.

God's promises to remember:

• Commit your works to the Lord and your thoughts.
Will be established (Proverbs 16:3, NKJV)

• I am the Lord your God, who teaches you to profit, who leads
you by the way you should go. (Isaiah 48:17, NKJV)

• For we are God's handiwork created in Christ Jesus
to do good works. Which God prepared in
advance for us to do. (Ephesians 2:10, NIV)

CHAPTER 9

THE FOURTH STEP:
LISTEN AND FOLLOW GOD'S
INSTRUCTIONS

T he fourth step of God's priorities for a successful happy life is to listen and follow His instructions. If you're a parent and you have children, it's the same thing you want them to do. If you're a teacher, it's what you want your students to do. If you're a coach, it's what you want your players to do. Listening and following God's instructions is the most important thing we can do to having good success and happiness in our life. On the other hand, when we choose not to listen and follow His instructions, we are rebelling against God and His plans for our life, which ultimately angers Him like his children Israel constantly did. The same way we feel when our kids don't listen to our instructions and do their own thing, they're rebelling against our authority. The bible tells us the first commandment about man is for children to listen and obey their parents. God wants us to start practicing that when we're children as soon as possible, especially the words "No" and "Ask first." I don't know about you, but those were the words I hated to hear the most when I was a child. That is the main reason I couldn't wait to be an adult and get my own place. I didn't want to hear the word "No" or to have to ask first. I wanted the freedom to do what I wanted when I wanted without having to ask at all. I believe that's what we all want to do whether you're a child under your parents' authority or an adult under God's. I remember when I was a kid I loved Oreo cookies. Dipping them in milk, I could eat the whole pack at one time. Once I started, I couldn't stop and finally ate the whole pack and got in trouble with my mother a few times. The problem was my mother liked Oreo cookies too. The next day after she bought them, she noticed they were all gone. She was really upset to say the least. I had to replace the whole pack with my allowance money. After that, I had to start asking before I ate the cookies. I hated having to do that. The funny thing is when I was an adult and got my own place, I still loved those Oreos and milk. And I could have easily eaten the whole pack at once and without having to ask. But I didn't because I couldn't afford it, so I would only eat one row at a time. I will admit it was a nice feeling having the freedom of not having to ask, but at the same time realizing things cost money. The other word we don't like to hear as children or adults is the word no. Because it usually means we can't have something or do something which we really want. I know that's the word I and my wife use the most when we watch our grandchildren, and some need to hear it more than others. Especially when they're between two to three years old, when they start walking and touching things, it seems everything they're about to do requires at least two Nos in a row. I remember for a while calling our living room the No, No room. The truth and funny part of that is we're not any different as adults. We want to do things were not supposed to. And just because we don't hear the words No, No anymore as children, it still applies to us as adults. God tells us "No" in the Ten Commandments and many times throughout the New Testament. The word No from God is what took me the longest to learn and when He says No to something, He really means it and doesn't change His mind. As opposed to someone else saying no at first but doesn't always mean it. If you're good at manipulating, sometimes you can change that no into a yes if you badger someone long enough. The thing is when God says no, we can't manipulate Him. The only alternative is to disobey. When we disobey God's No list, it may seem like we're getting away with it for a while. But somewhere down the road, there's always going to be a consequence payment to be made. And no matter what scheme or angle we come up with, we can never change the outcome of when God says no. The only way we can change that is by taking heed and obeying it. For all you younger people who might be reading this, when I was young I used to think God was too busy to be watching me every second. The older I get, the more foolish of a thought I realize that was. He was busy all right, watching me and the whole universe at the same time. That's too much for my brain to comprehend, so I have learned the best policy for living a successful happy life is at a child's level. In other words, whenever you hear God say no to something, don't do it. Whenever you hear God tell you to do something, do it. In a nutshell, that's all you have to do. "To please, God" sounds easy, right? Here's the hard part of that: we must obey what we hear. I believe there are a lot of Christians who listen to what God has to say but fall short on the obeying part. It's not enough just to listen to what God says. We need to follow through and obey it. If you're a parent and have children, look at it from your perspective. Is it good enough that your children only have to listen to what you say, or do they have to actually obey you to receive your goodness? The bible gives us the answer: "Children, obey your parents in the Lord, because it's the right thing to do and the first commandment with a promise. And if we learn to listen and obey, things will go well with us that we may live a long and successful life." (Ephesians 6:1–3) In other words, God commands us to listen and obey the moment we can understand a command from our parents' voice. When we become adults, the only thing that changes is we listen and obey God's voice and commands instead of our parents. There are tons of benefits and blessings that God gives us for listening to His voice and obeying His commandments. The biggest one is success; in fact, He promises it in every aspect of your daily life. On the other hand, if we don't listen and obey His instructions, just the opposite is true. I had to learn that the long hard way. If you want to know all God's benefits for listening and obeying and His consequences for not, I would highly suggest you take the time to read Deuteronomy chapter 28. I call that the benefit and consequence chapter of the bible. After I read that chapter, it made me want to start listening and obeying God a lot more. I did not want to have any more part of the consequence category. God makes himself perfectly clear on what we need to do if we want to enjoy all his blessings in every aspect of our life. That is, we need to diligently listen to His voice and obey all that He tells us to do. That's why God speaks to us more about listening than anything else he tells us to do in the bible. Adam and Eve lost their perfect life in paradise because of it. King Saul and King Solomon both lost their kingdoms for that same thing. They listened and heard God's instructions; they just chose not to obey it and do things their way.

In James 1:22, he tells us the test of obedience is being a doer of God's word and not a hearer only. And it can't be said any better in the song they teach children in Sunday school. Trust and obey, for there is no other way to be happy; in Jesus is to trust and obey. We can sing that song a thousand times, but do we really do what it says? That verse sums up the core of this book and should be the priority of our life. In other words, there's only one true way to be happy: that is by trusting Jesus and obeying his instructions. King David is my favorite example because he was the most successful king in the bible. He wasn't perfect: none of us are. The difference is that David listened and obeyed God's instructions overall better than anyone. The bible says David did what was right in the eyes of the Lord. And turned not aside from anything that God commanded him to do all the days of his life except only in the matter of Uriah, Bathsheba's husband. (I Kings 15:5) I believe that's one of the main reasons God called him a man after his own heart, because of his obedience to listening and following his instructions. That's why I use him as an example a lot, as of what we should be doing every day. He woke up every single day waiting to hear God's instructions on what to do next. He said, "**Show me your ways Lord, teach me your paths.** *Guide me in your truth and teach me, for* *you are God my savior, and my hope is in you all day long."* (Psalms 25:4, 5, NIV) That's why David was so successful. He had God's priorities in the right order. God said, "***I will instruct you and teach you in the way you should go.*** *I will guide you with my eye."* (Psalms 32:8, NKJV) God promises to be our teacher and coach 24/7 if we're willing to do our part by listening and following his instructions. In other words, if you want to be the best at something, then you need to find yourself the best teacher/ coach. I don't know of anyone better than Jesus himself. He's the only one in this world who has the time and the ability to have his eye on you all the time. Even if you had all the money in the world, you still couldn't buy that kind of coaching. This reminds me about years ago when I was training and coaching my son for the Golden Gloves. I had been teaching him how to box since he was about four years old. When he turned sixteen, I asked him if he wanted to win the state championship. He said, "Yes." Before we even started training, I told him, "The first thing you need to do is trust me that I know what I'm doing. Second thing is you need to listen to my voice and follow my instructions right when I tell you to do something. Don't second-guess me. Don't hesitate; just trust me and what I'm telling you to do." The reason I told him that is in boxing, everything happens in split seconds. You don't have time to second-guess or hesitate unless you like getting hit. I said, "If you can do that and work hard, then you can win the state championship. That's what winners do." I learned that from boxing myself. I watched a lot of fathers train their sons and they all became champions. At our gym, I had the privilege and opportunity to watch and train with some of the best boxers in the world such as Floyd Mayweather Jr., Buster Mathis Jr., and Tony Tucker. I noticed that all the fathers had different styles and training techniques. But there was one thing that they all had in common. They always had their eye intensely on their son, watching them every second for their mistakes and giving them the right instructions. That's when I realized that was the key to their success to becoming a champion. So I copied what they did with my son and he won the state heavyweight championship at sixteen. By beating the former two-time champion and still biggest boxer I had ever seen, weighing over 375 lbs., they called Big Buddha. I remember the commentators didn't give my son much of a chance at 6 feet 235 lbs. compared to that giant. I could see my son was a little intimidated when he got in the ring with Big Buddha. I had to build his confidence up. I told him before the fight, "Do you trust me?" He said, "Yes." I told him, "You have the skills to beat this guy. All you have to do is stick to the plan, listen and follow my instructions," and he did. The point I'm trying to make with this boxing example is what it takes to be successful in the ring is the same thing it takes outside the ring. I call it the boxing ring of life and you're in one corner of that ring whether you like it or not. And you're fighting the same opponent in the other corner every day. And who is that opponent? The bible says it's your adversary the Devil, and if you don't learn how to defend yourself against him, he's going to win every time. We can't run or hide outside the ropes of this life. You either learn to stand up and fight back or get beat up by the Devil. The apostle Paul said, "I'm in a spiritual fight" but not as though I'm punching the air at nothing: I know who my opponent is. As I said earlier, I'm a fighter and once I realized I was letting the Devil kick my butt, it made me angry. I said, "That's it, I'm going to learn how to spiritually fight back." That's when I asked Jesus to be my personal trainer/coach and claimed Psalms 32:8. We all need Jesus as a personal trainer/coach to teach us how to fight the Devil and guide us through this life if we want to win and have good success. Otherwise, how are you able to see your own mistakes and know the best way to correct them? David says the same thing about life: "**Who can understand his errors?**" (Psalms 19:12, KJV) The answer to that is we can't. That's why David had God as his personal coach. Let me ask you this question: do you have a personal life coach you can trust? Do they have the ability to have their eye on you 24/7, teaching and guiding you in the right way? If your answer is no, then you need Jesus because he is the ultimate best father, trainer, and life coach you could possibly have. He is the Son of God and the creator of all things. How do you get better than that? We can't, and the best part is his services are free and available to everyone who calls upon his name regardless of the situation. Especially all of you who don't have an earthly father to show you the right way. We would all like to have that advantage; unfortunately, a lot of us don't, biologically speaking. The good news is you don't have to live life with that excuse anymore like I did. Jesus says "I will be the father to the fatherless"; the only thing you have to do is be willing to listen and follow his instructions. Jesus promises and is ready to fulfill that void in your life if you let him. Jesus says, "I stand at your heart's door and knock and if anyone hears my voice and opens the door, I will come in and be with him." (Revelation 3:20) In other words, there are no excuses for the fatherless or any of us. Why? Because Jesus' office is never closed, his doors are open 24/7. And on his office door it says, "*I am the way, the truth, and the life and no man come's to the father except through me.*" (John 14:6, NIV) In other words, Jesus is not only our Lord and Savior, he wants to be your life coach too. If you want to know what the right way is, then listen to Jesus. If you want to know what the truth is, then listen to Jesus. If you want to know how to have good success and enjoy this life, then listen and follow Jesus. To all those who don't have an earthly father for whatever reason: it may not seem like you don't have the same advantage in life as those who do. That's because that's what the Devil wants you to believe. The truth is you do have a better advantage. We can't do any better than getting our instructions firsthand from our heavenly Father's Son himself. If you practice listening to Jesus' voice and following his instructions and plans for your life, you will always have the advantage like David. It does not matter how big the obstacle in front of you is. The difference between your earthly father and your heavenly Father is your earthly father can't always promise successful outcomes in your life like God can. Joseph and David didn't have their fathers right there instructing them what to do next: it was God. They started listening and obeying his instructions when they were teenagers and continued throughout their life till their death. Look at what advantage and favor God gave them. You can have the same thing too if you're willing to listen and follow instructions.

Do you need to slow down and listen?

God's ways are always one step at a time, one thing at a time, and one day at a time, and that's the way He wants us to live our life. In other words, to live that way, you can't be in a hurry all the time like I once was. That's why this step for me learning to slow down and listen to Jesus' voice was the hardest thing in the world for me to do. My reason was I didn't have anyone to teach me other than Jesus himself. And even if I did, my wife said I was too extreme and in a hurry to listen to anyone, much less God. She's been trying to tell me that our entire marriage. And that was probably God trying to speak to me through her all that time, but I didn't want to listen. To tell you the truth, I hated listening to anything that took more than 20–30 seconds, because listening requires you to slow down, sit still, and pay attention. I have ADD and a very short attention span; that's one reason I didn't read the bible or anything that I didn't absolutely have to. The only time I would listen to anything is if I knew it was going to benefit me in some quick way. My wife best describes me once as self-absorbed, extremist, always-in-a-hurry, and the worst listener in the world. I hate to admit that but it's the truth. That's how I lived my life until about ten years ago. What happened was I had all three steps down pat and I thought that was it at that time. Then I started praying and asking God what the next step was that he wanted me to do. That's when I started to hear the Holy Spirit telling me I needed to slow down and listen. When I heard that the first time, I really didn't want to believe that was God talking to me. At first, I ignored it and thought it might be my imagination and with time it would stop. I still kept praying the same thing, asking him what he wanted me to do next. I would hear the same answer: "You need to slow down and listen." I tried to act like I wasn't really hearing it and every time, that still small voice would get a little louder. That's when I started to realize this has to be God's voice. It couldn't be my imagination anymore. Why would I tell myself I needed to do that when I didn't like to do either one? I couldn't tell you how many times I heard I needed to slow down and listen. It was and still is the most repetitious thing God has ever said to me. I think I heard that for about two years. It was like He had it on auto record: every time I called, I got the same message. I heard it so much I wrote it down on my daily goal sheet as a spiritual priority and that's how it became the fourth step. About that same time in my life, my daughter saw the way I was hurrying and running around. She told me I needed to slow down or I was going to have a heart attack. I just laughed and said her mother's been trying to tell me that for years. I didn't listen to either one of them. Now I see why God had to speak to me directly because I wasn't listening to Him speak through my family. When you hear your daughter, wife, and God telling you to do the same thing at the same time, that's when I knew I needed to make another change in my life about slowing down a bit. When you're used to going 100 miles an hour, every day dropping down to 50 was big deal for me. (Figuratively speaking, not in a car.) The first thing I noticed is I could see and hear things a lot better when I started to slow down. That's when the Holy Spirit started showing me scriptures in the bible about listening to God's voice. Back then, the one that impacted me the most was when Solomon reminds us that when we talk to God, we need to be more ready to listen than to give sacrifice. And not to be quick in your heart to utter anything before God. "*Be more ready to hear, than to give sacrifice of fools. For they consider not that they do evil. Be not rash with thy mouth and let not thine heart be hasty to utter anything before God. For God is in heaven and thou upon earth. Therefore, let thy words be few. For a dream cometh through a multitude of business, and a fool's voice is known by multitude of words.*" (Ecclesiastes 5:1–3, KJV) In other words, it's more of a priority to listen to God than to do a whole lot of talking. I guess that's why God made us with one mouth and two ears. When I read it the first time, it cut right to my heart. I felt like He was talking directly to me. When God says you're a fool for not listening, in my opinion it is the worst thing to be called in the bible. Any time God says you're a fool for doing anything, it is serious. That's the time to take notice and make a change, because He has no tolerance for fools. That's when I started to slow down and practiced listening to Him more than talking. I believe that scripture is saying God has more to say to us than that we have to Him. Since then, I've learned if you don't take the time to listen to Jesus voice, you will miss out on a lot of good things. As crazy as this sounds, I used to hurry with God on a day-to-day basis and expected Him to follow me and listen to my voice when I wanted or needed something. Just like children try to do with their parents in the stores. I remember one day I was hurrying across a parking lot and told God, "Thank you for allowing me to move faster than most people." I couldn't believe his answer. He told me I was acting like a fool. The funny thing is my wife used to tell me that all the time and it never bothered me. But when you know it is God saying it to you, it's a whole lot different. So I said, "Why am I a fool for wanting to hurry? I thought it was good exercise." He didn't buy it. His answer was: "You're foolish because you're missing out." I said, "What is it I'm missing out on?" He said, "A lot of things. When you slow down and listen to me, you will find out." I didn't understand what I was missing out on back then but I wanted to, so I started to slow down. Now many years later, I understand what he was talking about. It wasn't any one thing: it was a whole lot of things. For instance, a big change for me, God wanted to teach me, is helping other people. When I started to slow down, I started noticing more people around me who needed help in some way and I would stop and take the time to help them. When I was in a hurry, I wouldn't see that opportunity or if I did, I wouldn't take the time to involve myself. That's because I was always in a hurry mood, thinking about myself over others for no other reason than to get from point A to point B as fast as I could. When I started to slow down, I found myself able to listen to God more and Him showing me all kinds of good things I would have otherwise missed out on altogether. I realize most people are not as extreme as I was and don't need to slow down. What I do know is we all need to listen and obey His instructions. We do that by tuning in to Jesus' station, his voice (the Holy Spirit). And if you're not tuned in to his station, you can miss that moment, that opportunity or experience that will pass you by and may never return again. God does not hold back or repeat time just so we can have another shot at that same opportunity. All we can do is learn from it as time ticks away from us, to never return again like water under a bridge. As I look back, what I regret the most were those things I missed out on when I was too much in a hurry to listen. If you're someone like I was, I can boldly say the same thing God said to me: you're living foolishly. Because you're missing out on a lot of good things in life he wants to show you—most importantly His purpose, plans, and direction He wants you to go. That's why it should be a priority to always be tuned in to Jesus' station; then you won't miss out on anything.

Are you tuned in to Jesus's station or something else?

Are you allowing the things of this world to distract you from being tuned in to Jesus? I believe that's the easiest thing we can allow ourselves to do, especially nowadays. In other words, look at all the devices we have that can easily eat up time and distract us from Jesus' voice and his presence. For example, smart phones is the number one thing you see no matter where you go. The majority of people I see don't have them in their pockets like they used to anymore. They have their phones in front of their faces and it hardly ever leaves their hands. Wherever there are crowds of people in airports, restaurants, events, etc., what do you see? To me it looks like a lot of people being controlled by a device as an antisocial group. I know most those same people are not really antisocial because a lot of them are trying to keep up on their favorite social media sites with their friends, and my wife is one of them. The point I'm trying to make is before smart phones, you could be waiting at those same places and you could at least make eye contact with the person next to you and strike up a conversation. Now they have their phones in their faces, texting a hundred miles an hour. And they're so focused on their phones you're afraid to say anything least you'd be interrupting them or looked at as being rude. In my opinion, the majority of the people who are socializing on their smart phones to an excess are becoming antisocial to the people around them without realizing it. That's how addicting it's become. And if that's the case, how much of the time is it causing you to be antisocial with Jesus when he's supposed to be your best friend? The question to ask yourselves is have you allowed that device to become the biggest distraction of your life? I want to make myself clear on this. I'm not saying there's anything wrong or bad with having a smart phone. I have one myself, but I don't have it in my hand or in front of my face all the time. If you're someone whose only time without a smart phone in your hand is when it's charging or when you're sleeping, would it be fair to say that's what you're tuned in to the majority of the time? If yes, you might be saying, "And what's so wrong with that?" The bible says anything that we do to excess is not good, whether it's abusing alcohol, drugs, smart phones, or eating honey. He that has no control over his own spirit is like a city that is broken down with no walls. (Proverbs 25:27, 28) In other words, God expects us to be in control of our life like a city with walls, not allowing anything to break in and control us, whatever that thing is.

Anything that we do to excess, that we let control our life other than God himself, is sin, therefore not approved by God. The apostle Paul says, "Be not drunk with wine to excess; instead, be filled with God's spirit to excess." (Ephesians 5:18.) Paul did not say drinking wine was sin; he said drinking it to excess is. In other words, Paul chose two extreme opposites of excess to make his point. That we should be filled with the Holy Spirit to excess more than anything else in our life; in this case, he chose getting drunk to excess in comparison. In other words, the only thing we can do to excess that controls us and is approved by God is being filled and controlled by the Holy Spirt. It took the majority of my life to figure that truth out, and I hope it doesn't for you. I used to do everything to the extreme and in excess—alcohol, drugs, wild parties, filthy language, workaholic, anger, bitterness, in trouble with the law, and jail. My wife, family and all my friends say I was the most excessive and extreme person they have ever met. In other words, I'm not proud about it. I've just had a lot of experience about excess in all the wrong ways, trying to find happiness. I can tell you this much: for sure you won't experience God's peace, joy, and happiness in anything you do to excess except to be filled with the Holy Spirt. To be honest, I never set out making it a goal to be filled with the

Holy Spirt. My goal was to be happy and successful God's way, following his steps. And when you listen and obey Jesus, it will ultimately lead you to be filled with his Holy Spirit.

A clean house makes room for the Holy Sprit

But before that happens, you have to clean house and get rid of all the excess in your life. In other words, if you don't get rid of all the garbage and excessive things you do in your life, the last thing in the world you'll be doing is listening to Jesus' voice through the Holy Spirit. That's because we become preoccupied with satisfying ourselves and distracted by all those things we allow into our life. Let's face it, we all have garbage in our life, some more than others. That's the only difference. In my case, I was so full of it to the point it overflowed into my family's life and others. I know that because I still hear about it now and then. The sad part is we don't see our garbage as being garbage as God and ever body else does in our life. This is why we need to listen to God, our family, and others; ask them if they see any garbage you need to get rid of.

If your life is full of garbage like mine was, it can be pretty overwhelming to know what to change. Imagine looking in your house and every room has garbage in it that you put there. And it's so overwhelming you don't know where to start. And as soon as you think about wanting to clean up your life, you will hear the Devil's voice telling you, "That's too much work. Just leave it where it is. Look, how long has it been there? It's not hurting anything." And that's a big fat lie. The truth is you're hurting yourself and those closest to you. On the other hand, if you listen to Jesus' voice, I can assure you he's going to tell you the truth and what room to start with. And when you're done with that room, he will tell you the next room and so on until your house is all clean. That's exactly the way he did with me, getting rid of the garbage and excess one room at a time, including slowing down. That's why it took the majority of my life: I accumulated a lot of garbage to clean up all at once. And when you finally get rid of all the excess and garbage, the Holy Spirit has room to fill every area of your soul. That's when you become filled with the Holy Spirit, which will then overflow into the life of your family and the people around you. The same way it does with the excess garbage. How do you know when you don't have any excess or garbage in your life? When the Holy Spirit stops pointing it out to you—and that might take a while depending how much of it you have to clean up. How long it takes is not important as getting started and staying with it until you're finished. The reason I chose the smart phone as an example of excess is based on what I see every day. In my opinion, that device is used to excess more than alcohol, drugs, or any one thing. I don't see the majority of people walking around drunk or on drugs, do you? My point here with the smart phone as with anything else is: does it control you or are you controlling it? God doesn't say we can't have and enjoy the things in our life, including smart phones. Just as long as that thing doesn't become excessive by replacing God's Holy Spirit and presence. Here's another boxing example: Floyd Mayweather Jr. undefeated retired world champion in my opinion so far is the smartest boxer ever. The reason is the one thing he would always say throughout his career I never forgot. He wasn't going to party, drink alcohol, do drugs, or let anything that would distract or prevent him from being at his best A-game. In other words, we should have that same kind of mentality, discipline, and focus towards God. Our ultimate goal and best A-game should be not to allow anything into our lives that's going to distract us or prevent us from the fullness of God's presence.

What's preventing you from God's presence?

Listen to what David says and one of my favorite verses: "*You will show me the path of this life. **In your presence is the fullness of joy,** at your right hand are pleasures for evermore.*" (Psalms 16:11, NKJV) In other words, we can never truly enjoy life to the fullest without God's approval and presence, because he won't allow it. The Devil knows that too and tries to get us to believe we can enjoy the things of this life without God's presence. Don't be fooled by that. Remember the Devil is a master of disguise and distractions. We all heard of the saying "Buyer beware," which means it's up to the buyer to examine what they're about to buy and assume all risk. The bible says Christians should beware in the same way, because Satan himself can be transformed into an angel of light. (II Corinthians 11:14) In other words, if Satan is able to disguise himself as an angel of light, then he's easily able to disguise himself as anything in this world. You might be saying if the Devil is that good at disguising himself, how do I know if what I'm doing is from him? The answer to that is listen to the Holy Spirit I call Jesus' station. When you're tuned into him, he reveals the truth because he is the truth. I say it this way: the Devil can fool us a lot of the time, but he can't fool the Holy Spirit. The key here is to examine yourself and your priorities. What are the things in your life that are distracting or preventing you from God's presence and hearing his voice? If you ask Jesus, the Holy Spirit will let you know what you need to stop doing or change. It may not be what you want to hear at first, but one thing is for sure: it will be for your best. All you have to do is listen and obey what he tells you. Jesus says, *"My sheep hear my voice, and I know them, and they follow me."* (John 10:27, KJV) In other words, to follow Jesus, we need to be tuned in and ready to hear his voice every day. If you can't hear his voice, how will you know how to follow his instructions on what to do next?

In case this might be new to you and you're saying, "How do you listen to Jesus' voice?" the first step is you need to know him as your personal Lord and Savior. You do this simply by asking him to forgive you of your sins and accepting him into your heart and life to be your Lord and Savior. Jesus says, "I know them, and they know me." Now you have a relationship. You can listen and talk to each other the same way you would in any intimate relationship. The only difference is it's not physical: it's spiritual; otherwise, everything else is the same. You may be a new Christian or maybe have been a Christian for years like myself and never was taught how to tune in to listen to Jesus. If that's you, I hope by the time you finish this book you will know and that it will change your life like it has mine. When I was a young Christian, I knew about the Holy Spirit and how to talk to God. As far as listening to his voice goes, I had not a clue on how to go about that. That topic is not spoken about as much as it should be. That's why it's so important to study God's word, because we can't live long enough to hear it all. In this fast-paced world we live in, our life can become full of distractions very easily and quickly. And before we know it, we're consumed by it all. And here is the problem: when we allow distractions and sin in our life to control us, we can't hear God's still small voice. The other side to that problem I learned is: God will not yell or raise His voice over our distractions just so you can hear Him. The key to listening to His voice is us tuning in to Him by tuning out everything else that distracts us. That's why he said, *"**Be still and know that I am God.**"* (Psalms 46:10, KJV) In other words, God is not telling us to slow down here: he's telling us to stop, listen, and acknowledge him without any distractions. For example, did you ever try talking with someone on the phone with loud music and people talking in the background? And when you can't hear the other person clearly, you try to find a quieter place to listen better without the distraction? In other words, we need to give that same respect of listening to God in our everyday life as best as we can. I know it's not easy and can't be done all the time, but that should be our goal. Like the old days with the AM/FM radios, every time you moved it to a different location, you had to retune it in, so you could hear the station you were listening to more clearly. That's what we need to learn to do: to constantly stay tuned in. Because every time we move, there's a new set of distractions around us. This is a skill that takes a lot of practice and not always easy thing to do. When I started to listen and obey God's voice, my life started to rapidly change for the best and it will for you too. The first thing I learned about listening to His voice is He can speak to us in many different ways. I have found there are five common ways God speaks to us. First is through his word, second is the Holy Spirit, third is directing of our thoughts, fourth is our family and others. Fifth is circumstances he allows to change the direction we're heading in our life.

In my experience, the primary and most common way He speaks to us is by reading and hearing of His word and the Holy Spirit. The bible says, "*For the word of God is quick and powerful and sharper then than any two-edged sword,* piercing even to the dividing asunder of soul and spirit and of the joints morrow. And is discerner of the thoughts and intents of the heart." (Hebrews 4:12, KJV) That's why we covered the importance of reading God's word in the first step. If I didn't read and study His word, I wouldn't have learned any of Jesus' steps.

The Holy Spirit is God's direct line

In this step it's about listening to Jesus' voice through the Holy Spirit. Jesus says, "*The Holy Spirit whom the father will send in my name, will teach you all things and remind you of everything I have said unto you.*" (John 14:26, NIV) In other words, the Holy Spirit is our teacher and communication station from God. That's why we need to be tuned in to His station the majority of the time to hear His voice and instructions—just like the telephone is to us as our main way of communication. Recently, hurricane Marie devastated Puerto Rico. Their biggest problem was communication. Over 80 percent of the country was without power and communication, which slowed down the rescue and relief process and help. That's one thing we don't ever have to worry about with our communication with God. No matter what storms hit us in this life, God promises us the Holy Spirit line will never be down. He said "I will never leave you or forsake you"; in other words, He's always going to be there. God has the best communication system on the planet. And I believe a lot of Christians don't take advantage of it as much as they should. Let's look at some of the benefits of the Holy Spirt. Best of all, it's free the moment you accept Jesus as your King and Savior. Think about it: we have direct access to the King of Kings and Lord of Lords. We can't just pick up the phone and call the president and even if it were possible, we would have to go through all kinds of protocol first. We have direct access to God through the power of the Holy Spirit 24/7 with no protocol. His line is never busy and you don't even need a device: it's been installed in you by God Himself.

And here's the part I like: it's FREE! And you never have to worry about recharging, upgrades, breaking, losing it, insurance, running out of minutes and data, dropping calls, roaming charges, changing plans for a better rate. It's 100 percent waterproof: you can go in the water as long as you want and deep as you want. In other words, its hands-free: you can drive your car having your eyes on the road every second. You can actually make eye contact with other people while you're tuned into the Holy Spirit. All the benefits and promises of God comes through His direct line the Holy Spirit, our healer and giver of gifts. All we need to do is realize it's installed in us and use it more than everything else in our life. The smart phone can give us directions how to get from point A to B in our car—most of the time anyway. The one thing it can't do is tell you how to do that in your life according to God's plan; only the Holy Spirit can do that. No matter what the technology age we live in, man will never come up with a better device than what the Holy Spirit can do for you. The only thing that can damage the performance of the Holy Spirit is by allowing and practicing sin in our life. The Holy Spirit's job is not only to teach and guide us through this life, but it's also there to convict and warn us of sin. That's why the bible tells us not to grieve and sadden the Holy Spirit of God. (Ephesians 4:30).

Whose voice are you listening to?

God didn't create us to be robots. He allows us choice and two stations and voices to listen to: Jesus' voice or the Devil's, and when we're not tuned in listening to Jesus, we default by nature and start listening to the Devil's station without even realizing it. Ever since Adam and Eve, nothing has changed except technology. They had two voices to listen to then and it's the same two we have today. God's voice and the Devil's—that's it, there are no other voices. And we all wake up to that same situation every day. And I don't believe the majority of Christians look at living life that way, yet it's still the truth. That's the way the Devil wants it to be. He doesn't want you to think you're listening to him. He wants you to think you're listening to yourself and that's a big lie. Eve wasn't listening to herself: she was talking with the Devil. I spent most my Christian life listening to the Devil's voice without really knowing it. You might be saying, "How do you know the difference between the Devil's voice and God's?" This is a very important question and one you may want to highlight. The difference is God's voice will never tell you to do something contrary to his word; that's why we need to read it and know it.

It's been said knowledge is power and that's true; in other words, the more knowledge about God you have, the more power you have over the Devil. And the reverse is true: the less knowledge of God you have, the more power the Devil has over you. I thought everything I did was my idea and my plan when I was living on the wrong road. And maybe it was a lot of times, because I don't think the Devil had to be too tricky with me back then. In other words, I was tuned into his station: he already had me as a listener. When I came up with a bad idea, all he had to do was say, "Good idea; go ahead, it will all work out," and pat me on the back. The truth of the matter is when we listen to ourselves with our plans and ideas, we're listening to the Devil's station. If you find yourself bored and talking to yourself, I'll warn you the Devil's right behind you listening to your thoughts. Why do you think they say the idle mind is the Devil's playground and workshop? The reason is when our minds are inactive and not tuned into Jesus' voice and instructions, we're allowing the Devil to propose to us his plan which is always an evil plan that ends in destroying your life. Boredom, idle mind, and constantly thinking about your own ideas are the tools the Devil uses. And I had all three of those things going on in my life until I started tuning in and listening to Jesus. Here's how it works: God has a plan as we discussed earlier, and this plan is carried out through the Holy Spirit, which teaches us our daily assignments. The Devil will use every tool in his workshop to distract and break that communication between you and God. The way to avoid that from happening is you being aware of that, which is half the battle. The other half of the battle is discipline and training yourself to listen to Jesus' voice. When we're tuned in to listening and following

Jesus every day, we're allowing him to show us his plan. There is no time for boredom, idle mind, and thinking about your own ideas. When we listen and follow Jesus, all those thoughts get wiped out. That's because when you take the tools away from the Devil, he doesn't have anything to work with. As long as you're tuned in listening to Jesus, you shut the Devil right down: he's out of business in your life. He has to flee from you when you stop listening to him. You're no good to him anymore. He has to pack up and get out of your life and set up shop in someone else if he sees you're committed to following Jesus. But always be aware he's never too far away. He does pop in now and then just to check on you, testing your commitment and allegiance to God. He won't hang around as long as you don't give him any reason to stay.

God's gentle whisper

I want to close this chapter with, in my opinion, the most difficult way we listen to God's voice. That's when He speaks to us in His gentle quiet voice that's like a whisper. I say it's difficult because if you're not listening or distracted by something, you're not going to hear it. That's why I repetitively say we need to be tuned in. Anything we want to hear that is important to us, we tune in to and or turn the volume up. The only problem with God's gentle whisper is we don't have a volume knob to turn it up. I asked God once about that. I said, "Could you speak just a touch louder, so I know it's you and not me?" His answer was, "You just need to listen a little harder," and I never asked him that again. In other words, God is not going to raise His voice

It's like having a radio with no volume control, only a tuner. The only way to hear that kind of radio is make sure it is perfectly tuned in and put your ear next to the speaker. That's my best analogy. I think one of the best lessons in the bible about distractions and listening to God's still small voice is found in I Kings 19:9–13. When God was teaching Elijah about listening to his quiet little voice, He told Elijah to stand back and watch the Lord as he demonstrated this lesson. The bible says when the

Lord passed by, there was a great strong wind which broke the mountains in pieces and rocks fell. But the Lord did not speak in the wind. Then there was an earthquake and the Lord did not speak in the earthquake. And after the earthquake, there was a fire, but the Lord did not speak in the fire either. And after the fire when everything was quiet, the Lord spoke with a gentle whisper. Elijah heard it and listened to the rest of God's instructions and direction on what He wanted him to do next. I can't imagine being in Elijah's shoes that day. That had to be the ultimate learning course for listening to God's quiet voice. Elijah could have easily been afraid and distracted by all that, yet he stood still and tuned in. The lesson to learn from that is first of all, God purposely caused those loud and visual distractions. Then he chooses not to speak during none of it until it was over and totally quiet. In other words, God chooses not to speak to us while we're distracted or compete with even his own distractions with a louder audible voice. If we want to hear his quiet little voice on what to do next in our life, then we need to follow that same example God showed Elijah: stand still and listen. That means we need to take some undistracted times out in our daily life. Since God has been teaching me how to listen to his quiet little voice, I realize now why he doesn't speak to us in a louder audible voice. The reason is if we heard God speak to us that way, we would fall down on the ground face first. For example, in Matthew 17:1–7, the time Peter, James, and John were standing and talking with Jesus, Moses, and Elias on a high mountain. A cloud overshadowed them, and they heard God's audible voice out of the cloud say, "This is my beloved son who I am well pleased, Listen to him." And when the disciples heard it, they immediately fell down on their faces and were very afraid. Then Jesus walked over, touched them, and said, "Get up. You don't need to be afraid. That's my father talking." The same thing happened with Abraham one time when he heard God's audible voice. The bible says he fell on his face as God talked with him. I believe that's one reason why he speaks to us in a gentle whisper. Think about it: if you were outdoors and you heard God's voice come from the clouds calling your name, your first reaction would be to fall down, the voice scaring the life out of you like it did the disciples and Abraham. Since we're talking about this, I can't help but tell this funny story I did to my wife years ago. This was not planned. It was a spontaneous moment that I couldn't help myself from taking advantage of. We have a 30 ft. pine tree in our front yard. One day I was putting Christmas tree lights on it. I had to climb up to the top to start the first row of lights. While I was up, there my wife pulled into the driveway from work. She did not know I was at the top of the tree, so in a few split seconds, I thought it would be funny to see how she would react if I said her name with a loud low voice like it was God calling her name down from the sky. When she got out of the car right below me, I yelled her name. Her first reaction was she squatted down holding her head like something was falling on her. I was laughing so hard I almost fell out of the tree and probably some of you ladies reading this think I should have. At first she didn't think it was funny until I told her why I did it, then she couldn't help but laugh about it too. That was a once-in-a-lifetime moment I couldn't resist. Getting back to the story, what we can learn from both Elijah's experience listening to God's quiet little voice and the disciples hearing his audible voice, we need to remember two things. The first one is God knows we can't listen very well when we're distracted by things going on around us. Second, hearing his audible voice would scare the life out of us, making us afraid, and we can't listen very well either way. It reminds me when I used to discipline my kids, I would raise my voice and get loud. My wife would be right there telling me I need to lower my voice because I was scaring them to where they can't listen to what I'm telling them. That's another reason I believe he speaks to us in a quiet little voice: so it doesn't make us afraid to listen.

As I was writing and thinking of this fourth step of God's priorities, I had to ask God this question: if listening and following His instructions is so important, then why should this not be the first step instead of the last step? First, He reminded me that He is a God of order and priorities. And then He reminded me of how those four steps came about in my life. In other words, God did not reveal to me all four steps at once: it was one step at a time and over a period of many years. Then He revealed why it is not the first step: we don't listen and follow instructions from someone we don't know and trust first. And when He explained it to me that way, it made perfectly good sense and I hope it does to you. Jesus' four priority steps for success, peace, joy, and happiness are nothing new. They have always been there since the beginning and it's the same for us today. For example, we can see it in the lives of Noah, Abraham, Joseph, Moses, Joshua, David, and Paul. They were just ordinary men like us with a different purpose and plan to carry out. I noticed one thing they all had in common: they followed God's priorities for success: the four steps. They all trusted God, they were all committed, and most importantly, they listened and obeyed His voice and instructions. And they all became the most successful godly men in the bible, along with many others who did the same thing. On the other hand, the bible is full of unsuccessful stories of men whom God chose to carry out his purpose and plans. For example, King Saul and King Solomon could have been in God's hall of fame for success. But they fell short by not following the fourth step: they listened but chose not to obey. That's always been God's bottom line from day one till now: listen and obey my commandments. God even went as far as sending His only Son to be sacrificed a cruel death to wipe away our sins from his face, so we could be reconciled back to God to be the sons of God. In other words, God gives us a clean slate each day to start over with, giving us another chance to listen and obey his commandments. That's always going to be God's bottom line for His success, peace, joy, and happiness. In I Peter 2:21, he tells us that Jesus suffered himself for us, leaving us a perfect example that we should follow in his steps. I had to ask myself, "What steps is Peter talking about? He doesn't follow up with any examples. So I looked up the definition of step, which simply say's putting one foot in front of the other in the right order to move forward in the direction you want to go. I believe the steps Peter's talking about are these four core priority steps, because that's what Jesus did and taught. Jesus plainly tells us what the first step is: seek first God and His kingdom. The second step is to trust and love God with all your heart, soul, mind, and strength. The third step he taught was "If you want to follow me and be my disciple, you need to be totally committed. If you're not willing to surrender all, you cannot be my disciple." The fourth step he taught was "Listen to my words and my voice, and if you love me you will obey my commandments." Finally, Jesus' last words and last step you could call the fifth step was to his disciples in his great commission statement in Matthew 18:18–20. "Now I want you to go and teach all nations, baptizing them in the name of the Father, the Son, and Holy Spirt. Then teach them all things I have commanded you." In other words, Jesus not only wants us to follow these four steps in our own life, he wants us to teach others to do the same throughout the world by the example he taught us. The thing I love about the four steps is it's like a spiritual compass: it lets you know where you're at and what you need to work on. At the same time, it shows you what the next step should be in the right direction with God's success plan for your life. Before God showed me His priority steps, I had a plaque in my office that says, "The man who walks with God always gets to his destination. If you're a women, that applies to you as well. That sounded good to me that's why I bought it, but at the same time there was something missing about it that always bothered me. In other words, it had a positive ending but without any steps to get to that destination. That was really frustrating to me, so I started studying the bible, looking for the answers. And I asked God everyday what steps I need to take to get to my destination. That's how this all came about. God answered and showed me the right way one step at a time. Today twenty years later, I still have that same plaque sitting on my desk. The only difference is it doesn't bother me anymore. That's because I know what steps to follow to get me there. I still don't know where that future destination on earth is or where it's going to end up. Here's what I do know and what matters most: I don't look at that destination as any one specific destination like I used to. In other words, like it's some kind of one goal I need to reach. The way I look at it now is I believe God can have many destinations for us to go and many purposes to use us for to accomplish his perfect will. Our purpose, destination, and daily assignments are all part of God's will and his responsibility, not ours. That's why he wants us to surrender our will to him. And once we have done that, our part is to make sure we are on the right path by listening to Jesus and following his steps. I don't worry about my purpose, destinations, or daily assignments like I used to. Instead, I wake up ready each day to accomplish His will whatever that is by listening to and following Jesus' steps. Ever since I've been doing that, I have peace, joy, and happiness that I was always looking for in all the wrong ways. It's the best feeling in the world when you know God has a purpose and success plan for your life and you're following it step by step and day by day on the right road.

Are you ready?

What's most important and matters right now is: do you want to live your life that way? I hope your answer would be yes, and if so are you ready to get started? Read Matthew 24:44–47. Jesus tells us we should be ready doing his will at all times because we don't know the exact time we are going to see Him. Jesus sacrificed his life for you and set the perfect example of priority steps for you to follow. Jesus did his part, now it's up to us to do ours. He didn't come here to please himself: he came to seek and save those who are lost. In other words, without following Jesus' steps in our life, we are just that lost. It doesn't matter what you have done in the past or how messed up your life is right now, Jesus specializes in changing lives like he did mine. The key is getting started and staying committed to following his steps. With God it doesn't matter how you start out in life: it is how you finish with the time he allows you. If you're a Christian, the bible says one day we're all going to see Jesus face to face. Imagine for a moment what that day might be like, to see and hear the creator for the first time surrounded by all his glory. Like the hit song, I can only imagine what it will be like when your face is before me. What are you going to, say, feel, or do? I don't believe any one of us knows the answer to that till that time comes. The bigger question to ask yourself is: are you prepared and ready to meet Jesus? In other words, how are you living your life each moment and day? Are you living it for yourself—following your dreams and plans? Or are you listening to Jesus and following his steps and plans he has for your life? Jesus said, "Be ye ready to meet me at all times, because you don't know when that moment will be." If you want to imagine something between you and Jesus meeting for the first time, then imagine what that moment will be like having the confidence to look Jesus in the face and hear him say these words to you: "Well done, good and faithful servant." That has to be the ultimate accomplishment and moment of anyone's life: that you're ready. For example, imagine if you could go anywhere in the world that you thought was the ultimate place to see. And you could go free because someone else already paid for it. Now the only thing left for you to do is pack and get ready. My friend Jesus is the one who already paid for that ticket to that ultimate place with his blood. And it's not any place here on earth: you can see or even possibly imagine. It's going to be the moment you see Jesus in all his glory. My point is we wouldn't think twice about getting ready to see the most beautiful place in the world. Like when my wife and I went to Hawaii, we were so excited we were ready and waiting way ahead of time. As Christians, that's how we should be living our life every day: excited, ready, and waiting to see what Jesus has next in our life by following his steps.

Key Questions to ask yourself:

• Whose voice are you listening to?

• What's preventing you from listening to Jesus and following his steps?

• Do you want to hear Jesus say, "Well done, good and faithful servant"?

Key points to remember:

• Anything we do to excess is not approved by God, except for being filled with His Holy Spirit.

• God doesn't speak to the hurried and distracted mind.

• Listening to Jesus and following his steps is the key to success.

God's promises to remember:

• I will instruct you and teach you in the way you should
Go. I will guide you with my eye (Psalms 32:8, NKJV)

• My sheep hear my voice, and I know them
And they follow me (John 10:27, KJV)

• Be still and know that I am God. (Psalms 46:10, KJV)

SUMMARY

I f God can take someone like myself who once lived my life listening to the Devil and living on his road—self- absorbed, bitter, angry, unforgiving, filthy mouth, the worst listener in the world, and add alcohol, drugs, and wild parties to all that—and then to turn that extreme life around, teach me how to listen to Jesus and follow his steps 24/7, and to live a balanced successful happy life; and then have me write a book about it—blows my mind when I look back at it all. I still can't believe it; only God can do something like that. It's amazing what He can do when someone is willing to change and surrender their life to Him. I know one thing for sure: if God did that to me, he can do the same thing to anyone who is willing. And that is the key: are you willing to let God change your life for the best and show the plans he has for you? I hope your answer is yes; if so, that's the first step to move forward on how to live a successful happy life. I don't know you or about your situation in life right now. What matters most is that you're willing to listen and obey God's principles and priorities that are the same for all of us. The first thing to know is there's no life so messed up that God can't turn around and use for his glory. Remember nothing is too hard or impossible with God. I believe the first thing God wants us to do before following His four steps is to examine yourself. Do you have any unforgiven bitterness or anger towards anyone as we discussed earlier in chapter 3? If so, that's a top priority on God's list that needs to be taken care of ASAP. If we want to have a close relationship with God and expect to receive all His goodness, favor, and blessings, then we need to forgive others. Because bitterness and anger only Rob's you of his joy and happiness. The next thing to examine is what road you're presently living your life on as we discussed in chapter 2. You can't live on the Devil's road and expect God's blessings at the same time as I said earlier, unless you believe Jesus and the Devil are buddies. Are you tired of calling your own shots and ready to let Jesus take over your life? Do you have a forgiving heart? Do you want to live your life on Jesus' narrow road that leads to a successful happy life? If you said yes to all three, you're ready for Jesus' four daily steps.

Jesus' four daily priority steps for living a successful happy life

1st Step The first step Jesus says is to seek God and His kingdom first before anything we do, most importantly by reading His word. Then every day, work at obeying God's number one priority to Love him with all your heart, soul, mind, and strength (Mark 12:30) In other words, put Him first in every aspect of your life.

2nd Step The second step Jesus wants you to do is Trust him 100 percent with all of your heart. Don't try to figure out how everything is all going to work out, just trust and wait on him. And in all your plans and daily task, acknowledge him and he will direct your steps. (Proverbs 3:5,6)

3rd Step The third step Jesus wants you to do is to be 100 percent committed by surrendering all of your will to him. In other words, let him be in control of every aspect of your life. Your part is to commit all your work into his hands every day and he promises to direct your thoughts on what it is he wants you to do next. (Proverbs 16:3)

4th Step The fourth step Jesus wants you to do is tune in and learn to listen to his voice and follow his instructions. He said, "I will be the one who instructs you and teaches you on what you should do. I will guide you with my eye." (Psalms 32:8)

The model prayer

Then start your day like David did. He said, "Cause me to hear your voice in the morning. I put all my trust in you. Show me the way I should walk today and teach me to know your will. (Psalms 143:8, 10) In my opinion, that should be a daily model prayer that every Christian should be asking God for.

Conclusion

Jesus' four steps and the model prayer is what has changed my life many years ago. I still have these steps written down on a piece of paper as a bible marker. I used to look at it every day till it became a habit and part of my life. I can assure you if you do the same thing and follow Jesus' four priority steps, you'll start to see your life rapidly change for the best. Because now you have the steps to follow that will keep you connected to Jesus, so he can show you his awesome plans and purpose he has for your life. And as long as you stay connected to Jesus, you will experience his peace, joy, success, and happiness in all that you do.

CPSIA information can be obtained
at www.ICGtesting.com
Printed in the USA
BVHW041912160721
612173BV00015B/368

9 781400 327256